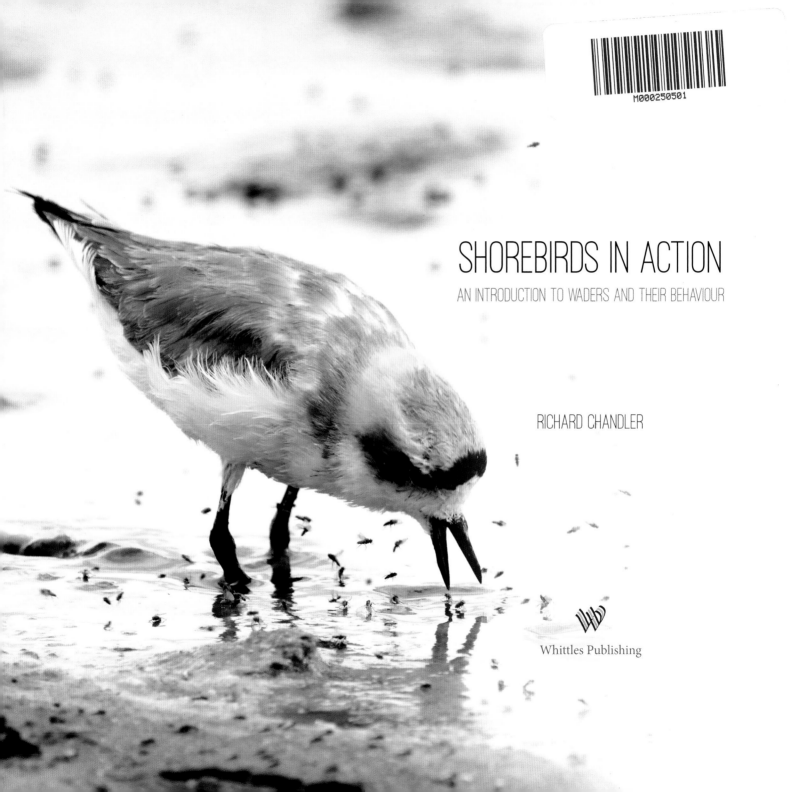

SHOREBIRDS IN ACTION

AN INTRODUCTION TO WADERS AND THEIR BEHAVIOUR

RICHARD CHANDLER

Whittles Publishing

Published by
Whittles Publishing,
Dunbeath,
Caithness KW6 6EG,
Scotland, UK

www.whittlespublishing.com

© 2017 Richard Chandler

ISBN 978-184995-355-9

Printed by Gomer Press

CONTENTS

INTRODUCTION

What is the particular appeal of shorebirds? This book attempts to answer that question.

Take a few random reasons as part of the answer. Shorebirds have evolved to occupy a surprising range of habitats worldwide, from the Arctic, through the tropics, to the Antarctic. They occur coastally, inland, on wetlands, in deserts, on open grassland and in woodland and forest. Many of these are wild places that appeal to those of us who have even a mild sense of adventure. Included amongst the shorebirds are the most extraordinary migrants of any animal species, which regularly fly for days at a time, covering thousands of kilometres. Many species have developed what are, even in these days of electronic sophistication, extraordinary sensing devices to find food below ground. Every spring they enliven the lengthening days with their dramatic in-flight displays and with their wonderful calls – even if the calls have to sometimes be interpreted as a stream of expletives! They have a surprising range of plumages, some species having the same appearance all their lives, others completely change their appearance every few months, matched by a surprisingly complex range of breeding strategies. And the list goes on.

My fascination with shorebirds started with an academic research expedition to high Arctic Spitsbergen in the early 1970s where I was involved in geotechnical engineering, not avian biology! At that time, it was not possible to fly there and a whole week beckoned on the 'fast' mail boat from Bergen, sailing north up the Norwegian coast, across the Barents Sea, past Bear Island, to the Svalbard archipelago – and I needed something to occupy my time. I had treated myself to a pair of binoculars a few months earlier, so the obvious solution was bird watching! My list of birds seen during the expedition was quite short, particularly in Spitsbergen itself, but it included a few shorebird species: breeding Grey Phalaropes; a single, off-route Red Knot (it was red, in full breeding plumage); and Purple Sandpipers, which confused me as they had darkish legs, despite the book I had with me implying that yellow legs were an important field mark. I later discovered that the field guide omitted to mention that their legs got darker in the breeding season!

A few months later, now with a real interest in shorebirds, a visit to the Isle of Sheppey in Kent, UK, again found me puzzling over shorebird identity – this time different species were involved, and they all looked confusingly similar. So similar in fact that I was not only confused, but even challenged, to put a name to them.

At about the same time I discovered the journal *British Birds*, which had recently published an article on bird photography. This featured photos of shorebirds by the husband-and-wife team Brian and Sheila Bottomley that showed how much could be learnt from high quality photographic images. I was hooked, both by the shorebirds themselves and now on photographing them. This book is one result.

The intention here is to describe and illustrate aspects of shorebird behaviour. Although this is deliberately not a shorebird identification guide, one criterion used for selecting the photographs is to show as many different species as possible. As a result, about 180 shorebird species are illustrated – around 80% of the world's total of 226 species – hopefully allowing this book also to be a useful identification reference.

A few images of other bird species are also included to show similar – or contrasting – behaviour to that of shorebirds.

The book is meant, in the context of its relatively compact size, to be read either as an introductory text on shorebird behaviour, or enjoyed as a series of photographs, showing that behaviour – but preferably both, accompanied by the captions that explain what is being illustrated. The reader who wishes for more detail on shorebird identification, plumages and ageing, as opposed to behaviour, should refer to texts such as my *Shorebirds of the Northern Hemisphere*.

Most of the aspects of a shorebird's life and behaviour are described here: plumages and moult, feeding, physiology and comfort behaviour, breeding, migration and flocking. It is well beyond the scope of a relatively small book to deal with all these topics on a species-by-species basis, and consequently the more detailed coverage is restricted to a relatively few species that are reasonably representative of the world's shorebirds. Examples are provided from Europe, Asia, Australasia, and both North and South America in an attempt to provide a survey that is as wide ranging as possible. The reader who is interested in taking the subject further is directed to the references at the end of this Introduction.

TERMINOLOGY

The seasons of the year in the northern hemisphere (and referring to northern hemisphere species) are used unqualified ('summer', 'winter', etc.); seasons in the southern hemisphere are given the qualifier 'Austral'. Short notes relating to the identification and ageing of individual birds are added at the end of many of the captions, together with the photographic location. Additionally, as shorebird plumages vary with the calendar, the month is also given, qualified as 'early' (1st–10th of the month), 'mid' (11th–20th) and 'late' (21st–end). But if this information is too much, skip those bits and just enjoy the photos!

The image right defines the various groups of feathers that are referred to in the text – kept to a minimum for sake of simplicity!

REFERENCES

Further reading on shorebird behaviour might include the following:

Chandler, R.J., 2009. *Shorebirds of the Northern Hemisphere*. Christopher Helm: London.

Colwell, M.A., 2010. *Shorebird Ecology, Conservation, and Management*. University of California Press: Berkeley, CA.

Cramp, S. and Simmons, K.E.L. (eds.), 1983. *The Birds of the Western Palearctic*, **III**, *Waders to Gulls*. Oxford.

del Hoyo, J., Elliott, A. and Sargatel, J. (eds.), 1996. *Handbook of the Birds of the World. Volume 3: Hoatzin to Auks*. Lynx Editions: Barcelona.

Hayman, P., Marchant, J.H. and Prater, A.J., 1986. *Shorebirds: An Identification Guide to the Waders of the World*. Croom Helm: London and Sydney.

van de Kam, J., Ens, B., Piersma, T. and Zwarts, L., 2004. *Shorebirds. An Illustrated Behavioural Ecology*. KNNV Publishers: Utrecht, The Netherlands.

ACKNOWLEDGEMENTS

I thank the following for help in various ways in producing this book. Ian Carter very generously offered to read the book in draft, and did so amazingly swiftly. John Dowding answered questions regarding shorebirds in New Zealand and, in particular, provided information on Shore Plovers and the valiant attempts being made to preserve them. David Fisher was very supportive on several occasions with my attempts at shorebird photography, and Simon Gillings provided me with several papers that I had difficulties locating. John Hunt very kindly commented on an early draft, and Chris Knights provided generous help with photography. Ian Newton was very encouraging during the early gestation stages, and on many occasions Danny Rogers provided useful mainstream

mantle

tertials

primaries

scapulars

wing-coverts

– and background – information whenever I needed assistance. David and Pat Wileman, who compile shorebird records for the Cley Reserve in Norfolk, UK, kindly provided data on various marked birds, particularly 'Blackwit' OG-OGflag.

But the greatest thanks go to my wife Eunice, who continues to pander to an obsessed shorebird enthusiast and, on this occasion, even helped out with last minute proofreading!

Madagascan Buttonquail, in typical dry, scrubby, buttonquail habitat.
Buttonquails are a group of small, skulking gamebird lookalikes –
this one is no exception – that have only recently been recognised as
members of the *Charadriiformes*. Madagascar, late November.

1 / INTRODUCING THE CAST

THE SHOREBIRD SPECIES

SHOREBIRD TAXONOMY

All science, at whatever level, needs to start with classification, and this book is no exception. Within the order *Charadriiformes*, in which the shorebirds are placed, the majority of current classification studies recognise three groups: the *Charadrii* (which include the stone-curlews, sheathbills, stilts, avocets, oystercatchers, plovers, lapwings, etc.), the *Scolopaci* (painted snipes, jacanas, curlews, the various sandpiper species, snipe and woodcocks, etc.), and the *Lari* (coursers and pratincoles, but also including skuas, auks, terns and gulls). The taxonomic relationships are not entirely clear, however, and, as a consequence, some authorities assign groups and species such as the buttonquails and Crab Plover to the *Charadrii*, while others place them in the *Lari*.

The sequence and English names of the shorebird species covered in this book follow that developed by the International Ornithological Congress (IOC). This list is given in the Appendix, page 244. The buttonquails, placed by the IOC at the beginning of the *Charadriiformes*, are only briefly mentioned here, while the skuas, auks, terns and gulls are families not generally regarded as shorebirds and are therefore not covered. This sequence is used, so far as is practical, within each chapter for both text and photographs.

In this chapter, all the various families or groups of genera are introduced in order to provide a framework for the subsequent discussions of shorebird behaviour.

BUTTONQUAILS AND QUAIL-PLOVER

The buttonquails (*Turnicidae*) have only relatively recently been included within the *Charadriiformes*. The systematics of the buttonquails has been much debated, with most authorities in the past putting them either with the true quails (*Galliforms*) or the rails (*Gruiformes*). It has recently become apparent, however, that they are members of the *Charadriiformes*, although visually they give every impression of being small game birds. They are sexually dimorphic, the females being slightly larger, with brighter and more colourful plumage than the males and, surprisingly for quite small birds, the females have an inflatable oesophagus that enables them to give a booming call.

There are 16 species of buttonquails, plus the Quail-plover (whose taxonomic position is enigmatic), distributed throughout the drier old world tropics and mid-latitude temperate zones of Africa, and from Southeast Asia to Australia. They are largely sedentary, although some species do make short-distance migratory movements, and they occupy dry grassland and woodland, a habitat not used by many shorebird species, except perhaps for thick-knees and woodcocks. Behaviourally they seem to have relatively little in common with the shorebirds and are therefore not discussed further.

STONE-CURLEWS AND THICK-KNEES (BURHINIDAE)

There are ten species of thick-knees (or stone-curlews) worldwide, in two genera, *Burhinus* and *Esacus*. All ten species are relatively large, although the two *Esacus* species and the Bush Stone-curlew are the largest. They are shorebirds of the tropics and temperate mid-latitudes, with two Central and South American species, and eight

[Opposite, upper left] Adult Indian Stone-curlew. Until quite recently this species was regarded as a race of the very similar Eurasian Stone-curlew. All stone-curlews and thick-knees are crepuscular and nocturnal, feeding at night and roosting by day. India, early January.

[Upper right] Senegal Thick-knee. Very similar to Eurasian Stone-curlew, but lacks a white bar on the folded wing. The Gambia, early January.

[Lower left] Spotted Thick-knee. An African species at its daytime roost. All the thick-knees have quite similar spread-wing patterns. Kenya, mid September.

[Lower right] Water Thick-knee, an adult on a wet afternoon. Superficially very like Eurasian Stone-curlew, but with proportionally longer bill, legs and tail. Kruger National Park, South Africa, mid November.

species distributed across Africa, Europe as far north as southern England, and South Asia to Australia. They are largely sedentary, apart from the Eurasian Stone-curlew, which has a relatively northern distribution and moves south in the winter within Europe – perhaps as far as north Africa.

The English names 'thick-knee' and 'stone-curlew' have been applied to most of the species at different times and by different authorities. The name 'stone-curlew' was originally applied to the Eurasian Stone-curlew in dual recognition of its nocturnal curlew-like calls and of its dry, stony, open-country habitat, whilst the term 'thick-knee' recognises its prominent tibiotarsal 'knee'. The name 'dikkop' is often used for the African thick-knee species. Most are birds of open country (Eurasian Stone-curlew, Spotted Thick-knee, Double-striped Thick-knee and Peruvian Thick-knee), although some favour dry open woodland (Indian Stone-curlew and Bush Stone-curlew), whilst others (Senegal Thick-knee and Water Thick-knee) prefer open river or lake-side habitats, and yet others (Great Stone-curlew and Beach Stone-curlew) are found on dry river-beds or coastal beaches.

All are largely crepuscular or nocturnal, and have noisy, far-carrying wailing calls at night during the breeding season. Their large eyes testify to their nocturnal habits; during the day they usually roost inconspicuously in tallish vegetation or under trees or bushes, feeding mainly at night.

The *Burhinidae* are largely similar in plumage and structure, with pale brown streaked or spotted plumage, although the two *Esacus* species have prominent black-and-white head markings. They all have yellow legs and quite short, almost black, bills often with a yellow mark at the base. Again, the two *Esacus* differ somewhat from the *Burhinus* species in having more massive, heavier bills.

The flight pattern of all species is quite dramatic and contrasts with the rather plain standing birds. With all but the Beach Stone-curlew, the primary and secondary feathers are black, with a prominent white flash on the inner primaries and gull-like white 'mirrors' at the wing tips. The Beach Stone-curlew differs in having all-white inner primaries and pale grey secondaries, although otherwise the

[Right] Bush Stone-curlew, a particularly long-legged stone-curlew, at its daytime roost under trees in a churchyard. Queensland, Australia, early September.

[Middle] Great Stone-curlew. One of the two *Esacus* species, both of which are large, with strong face patterns. In typical river-bed habitat. Uttar Pradesh, India, late December.

[Below] Beach Stone-curlew. The other of the two *Esacus* species. On the beach. It is tempting to wonder if it has deliberately aligned its wing pattern with the drift-wood in an attempt to be a little less obvious. Queensland, Australia.

flight pattern is similar to the other species. Some species (Eurasian Stone-curlew and Bush Stone-curlew) use the black-and-white wing pattern in a striking open-wing courtship display.

There is little sexual dimorphism, and in all species male and female are similar in size and structure, although some species show minor plumage differences when breeding, for example the males may show more black in the head or in the folded-wing pattern. This is particularly the case with the Eurasian Stone-curlew, where the white bar on the folded wing of the male has a much darker lower border than that of the female, and with the Double-striped and Great Stone-curlew, where the male can often be identified by its slightly blacker head pattern. Juveniles of all species are very similar to the adults, but are usually slightly paler, with less contrast in the head and/or folded wing patterns.

SHEATHBILLS AND MAGELLANIC PLOVER

There are two species of sheathbill, both occurring in the Antarctic and sub-Antarctic. They both have horny sheaths at the base of their bills that gives them their name, and both are scavengers and opportunist feeders, particularly at penguin or seal colonies. The monotypic Snowy Sheathbill breeds in Antarctica close to southern South America, to where many move when non-breeding. The Black-faced Sheathbill breeds on sub-Antarctic islands in the southern Indian Ocean. There are four races of the sedentary Black-faced Sheathbill, all visually very similar.

The Magellanic Plover is a small, aberrant plover that has plain grey upper parts and short bright pink legs. It has uncertain affinities, but seems to be most closely related to the sheathbills. It is rather turnstone-like in its feeding habits, probing with its bill amongst seaweed on the shore, but digging in sand with legs and feet, rather than using its bill as would a turnstone. It breeds at upland lakes in Tierra del Fuego, Argentina, and moves relatively short distances northward to coastal areas during the Austral winter.

OYSTERCATCHERS, CRAB-PLOVER AND IBISBILL

Oystercatchers are a group of 11 closely related species, with very similar plumages and behavioural traits. A twelfth species, the

Snowy Sheathbill. A scavenger at penguin and seal colonies. Tierra del Fuego, Argentina, early December.

Adult Magellanic Plover. The only member of the *Pluvianellidae*;
its closest relatives are the sheathbills. Tierra del Fuego,
Argentina, early December.

Canary Islands Oystercatcher, has not been reliably sighted since 1913 and is presumably extinct. The oystercatchers can be separated into two groups. First, the American species, all of which have yellow eyes: Magellanic, Blackish, American Black and American Oystercatcher; and second, those from the remainder of the world: African Black, Eurasian, South Island, Australian Pied, Variable, Chatham and Sooty Oystercatchers, all of which have red eyes. It is uncertain if the Mexican and South American subspecies of American Oystercatcher, *durnfordi*, *frazari* and *pitanay* (all three of which are identifiable in the field from a combination of flight pattern and the neatness or otherwise of the lower edge of the black breast-band), are clinal variations, introgressions between American, Blackish and American Black Oystercatchers, or good subspecies. The latter view is taken here. The geographical isolation of the Galapagos race of American Oystercatcher *galapagensis* points to that being a good subspecies.

All the oystercatcher species are very similar in structure, size, behaviour and habitat. Females are marginally larger and longer-billed than the males, although the body size difference is not usually apparent in the field. Once adult, oystercatchers of all species can usually be sexed on a combination of eye pattern and bill shape. Adult females have dark flecking on the iris adjacent to the pupil, making the pupil appear oval; adult males lack or have only minor flecking, making the pupil appear circular, or almost so. This is more easily seen on all the yellow-eyed American oystercatcher species, but it also seems to apply to all the red-eyed species. Although bill shape varies somewhat between the various oystercatcher species, the females have longer, slender, more tapered bills than the males, whose bills are somewhat deeper at mid length. If a pair (i.e. male and female) are seen together there is rarely any difficulty in assigning the sex to both birds. However, these pupil and bill distinctions can usually only be made with adults because the iris of immature oystercatchers of both sexes may be quite dark.

All juvenile oystercatchers have distinctive brownish-black plumage, and their eye and bare-part colours are initially dull and dark, but develop the brighter adult colours with age. All have

Magellanic Oystercatcher. In many ways this is the most 'different' of the world's oystercatchers; amongst other differences it is the only oystercatcher to have white secondaries. Southern Chile, late November.

Blackish Oystercatcher. As with other black oystercatchers, this is a bird of rocky coasts, the only black oystercatcher in South America. Tierra del Fuego, Argentina, early December.

orange bills when adult, but the legs of adults are creamy-flesh in the American species and pink in all the others. They are unusual for shorebirds in that the chicks are fed by their parents and continue to associate closely with their parents for two to three months after fledging (see Chapter 5). Oystercatchers take at least four years to reach maturity and breed.

The Eurasian Oystercatcher is the most numerous of the oystercatcher species. Indeed, the population of the nominate race alone exceeds the total population of all the other oystercatcher taxa combined. Eurasian Oystercatchers of races *ostralegus* and *longipes* are the only oystercatchers to have a distinctive non-breeding plumage. When they moult from their juvenile to first non-breeding plumage they acquire a broad white fore-neck collar that they retain until they reach breeding status in their third or fourth years. Thereafter, the white collar is only a feature of their non-breeding plumage, which they have from about October to February. It also seems likely that some of the oldest birds do not develop a white non-breeding collar and remain in breeding-type plumage year-round. Even at the height of the non-breeding season any reasonably large flock of the nominate race will contain about 5% of birds that have no white collar. At the eastern end of the range of the Eurasian Oystercatcher, race *osculans* gains at most a few tiny white throat feathers in its first non-breeding plumage. Another feature of this race is that it has the longest bill of any of the oystercatchers. These differences suggest that it may eventually prove to be a full species, rather than just a race of Eurasian Oystercatcher.

Behaviourally, all oystercatchers are very similar: all have piping displays in which they hold their bills vertically downwards, and give high-pitched far-carrying rapidly repeated calls, often by two or more birds together. This display is territorial and may be given at any time of the year, but most frequently at the commencement of the breeding season.

The adult Magellanic Oystercatcher shares the yellow eye and pale creamy-flesh leg colour of the other American oystercatchers, but differs from the other oystercatchers in several respects. It has a yellow orbital ring (the other species all have orange or red

African (Black) Oystercatcher. Perhaps the shortest billed of all the oystercatchers, its small population is restricted to coastal southern Africa. Male left, female right; note the pale orange orbital ring of this species. South Africa, early November.

[Right] Eurasian Oystercatcher. A pair of the eastern race *osculans*, female right and male left. This race has the longest bill of all oystercatchers and, unlike the western races, immatures do not develop a white collar (but see page 8). South Korea, early May.

[Middle] Australian Pied Oystercatcher. Queensland, Australia, early September.

[Below] Variable Oystercatcher. A female, with long slender bill and apparent oval pupil. This species has two colour phases: an all-black phase and a pied phase (as here) that has variable amounts of black below, depending in part on age (see also page 181) South Island, New Zealand, late January.

Chatham Oystercatchers. Another 'classic' pied oystercatcher, although rather short-legged, whose small population is confined to the Chatham Islands that lie east of South Island, New Zealand. Late November.

[Upper] Sooty Oystercatcher. There are two races of this Australian species. This is race *opthalmicus* of northern and north-western Australia that has a particularly large, fleshy orbital ring and black, not pale, claws. The nominate race *fuliginosus* occurs coastally in south and south-east Australia. Northern Territory, Australia, mid September.

[Lower] Sooty Oystercatcher, race *fuliginosus*; compare with previous photo. Victoria, Australia, early September.

orbital rings), its secondaries are virtually all white (not largely black as in the other species), it is the only American species with black rather than brown-black upper parts, and its chicks share plumage details with the old world oystercatcher species which differ from those of the other oystercatchers of the Americas. It also has a unique piping display in which it cocks its tail upward and gives the usual piping calls, but at times will give very high-pitched, almost 'electronic' calls, quite unlike any other species of oystercatcher.

The various black oystercatchers are all birds of rocky coasts. The American species (Blackish of South America and American Black of the North American Pacific coast), as with the pied American Oystercatcher, have brown-black upper parts, while the upper parts of the other black species (African Black, Variable of New Zealand and Sooty of Australia) are truly black. The Variable Oystercatcher, endemic to New Zealand, is unique in that it has two colour phases: either black at all ages or a pied version, which has recently been shown to acquire an increasing extent of black feathering with age. African Black Oystercatcher, the shortest billed of all oystercatchers, is more-or-less restricted to the rocky coasts of west and southern South Africa.

The South Island (Pied) Oystercatcher is a typical pied oystercatcher, often colloquially known as 'SIPO'. Endemic to New Zealand, it breeds inland in South Island, moving to North Island when not breeding. The Australian Pied Oystercatcher is very similar to the South Island Oystercatcher, with the two species differing mainly in flight pattern where the latter has a broader and longer white wing-bar and a white rump that extends in a 'V' up the back, which is more square in the Pied Oystercatcher. The Chatham Oystercatcher is a pied oystercatcher endemic to the New Zealand Chatham Islands, where it occurs coastally on both rocky and sandy coasts. In 2004 it had a total population of about 300. Although superficially similar to the South Island Oystercatcher, recent molecular analysis shows it to be a full species. The Sooty Oystercatcher of Australia is the other all-black Australasian oystercatcher, with two races that are separable in the field.

STILTS AND AVOCETS

There are five species of stilts in the genus *Himantopus* and one species, Banded Stilt, in the genus *Cladorhynchus*. The five *Himantopus* species are separated geographically and they also differ in their adult plumages. Adults of the Black-winged Stilt of southern Europe and Asia show a considerable range of different head and neck plumage patterns, which vary rather inconsistently with age, breeding status and sex. Occasionally they may even resemble other *Himantopus* stilt species. The adults of other *Himantopus* species all have consistent head and neck patterns. The Australasian Pied Stilt has a black hind-neck with a ridge of raised feathers and white shoulders. The North American Black-necked Stilt has a black hind-neck, as its English name suggests, with a small white patch above the eye; its subspecies 'Hawaiian' Stilt *knudseni* is also distinguishable in the field. Adults of the closely related White-backed Stilt of South America have a white hind-neck collar that separates the black hind-neck from the black back. The juvenile White-backed Stilt lacks this feature and is very similar to the juvenile North American Black-necked Stilt (see also Chapter 2, page 89).

New Zealand's endemic and critically endangered Black Stilt is indeed all-black as an adult, but immatures are initially pied and only become completely black after about two years. The total population is only about 100 individuals and it is one of the world's rarest birds, in spite of great efforts that are being made to preserve them. The major causes of the low numbers are introduced predators, such as European Stoat *Mustela erminea*, and the hybridisation with the closely related and far more numerous Australasian Pied Stilt. It only breeds in the Mackenzie Basin in South Island, where they are sedentary and where the population is supported by the release of captive-bred birds. The hybrid stilts are widespread throughout New Zealand.

The monotypic Banded Stilt of Australia is in many ways more similar to the avocets than to the *Himantopus* stilts. As with avocets, it has a bill with lamellae for filtering food items and strongly webbed feet, neither of which the *Himantopus* stilts possess. It also differs from the other stilts (and all avocets except the American Avocet) in having a distinct breeding plumage: the

Crab Plovers, juvenile (left) and adult. As its name suggests, the massive bill enables it to specialise on crabs as prey. Madagascar is about the southern limit of its non-breeding range from its Arabian Gulf breeding area. Madagascar, early December.

[Opposite] Ibisbill. An iconic shorebird of Himalayan valleys whose closest relatives are the oystercatchers. Uttar Pradesh, India, early January.

[Right] Australasian Pied Stilt. The world's stilts are all very similar, although with different head and neck patterns, but the Australasian Pied has a ridge of feathers running down its hind neck. New Zealand, mid November.

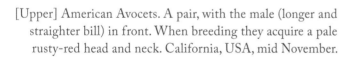

[Upper] American Avocets. A pair, with the male (longer and straighter bill) in front. When breeding they acquire a pale rusty-red head and neck. California, USA, mid November.

[Lower left] Black Stilt. As for several of the New Zealand shorebirds, this is one of the world's most endangered birds whose population is maintained only with a captive breeding programme. South Island, New Zealand, early February.

[Lower right] Black-necked Stilt. A female, with slightly bronze-brown (not black as with males) upperpart feathers. California, USA, early November.

dark chestnut breast-band that gives the species its English name (see also Chapter 5).

There are four avocet species *Recurvirostra*, all monotypic. The Pied Avocet breeds from western Europe to central Asia, migrating south to winter in Africa, the Middle East and parts of south-eastern Asia. The American Avocet occurs in North America and the Red-necked Avocet in Australia, whilst the Andean Avocet has a restricted distribution in the Andes of Peru, Bolivia, Chile and Argentina. With care, breeding pairs of all four species can often be sexed on bill length and shape because males have longer, less up-curved bills than females – a difference that is most obvious with American Avocets. The American Avocet has a pale rufous head and neck when breeding, whilst the Red-necked has a dark chestnut head and upper neck year-round.

LAPWINGS

The lapwings and plovers can be placed in three groups: the lapwings, the *Pluvialis* plovers and a rather large and diverse group of smaller plovers.

There are 22 species of lapwing, all in the genus *Vanellus*. The Javan Lapwing has not been sighted since the 1930s and is presumed extinct. The lapwings are all large, long-legged, generally noisy shorebirds, three of which have crests (Northern, Black-headed and Southern Lapwings). The monotypic Northern Lapwing of Europe and Asia is the most widespread and numerous of the lapwings. Largely sedentary in the southern part of its breeding range, the more northerly birds move southward in winter. Although many of the other lapwings are largely sedentary, particularly the African species, other lapwings are migratory, including the Grey-headed Lapwing of East Asia, the Sociable and White-tailed Lapwings that breed in west and central Asia, and the Spur-winged Lapwing of the eastern Mediterranean. The Brown-chested Lapwing is notable for being a long-distance migrant within Africa (see Chapter 6). The Spur-winged Lapwing is confusingly named because at least eight lapwing species have prominent spurs at the bend of the wing! Africa is home to 11 of the lapwing species, a concentration that suggests that the genus may have evolved in Africa.

[Upper] Red-necked Avocet. A largely sedentary species that occurs only in Australia. Victoria, Australia, late August.

[Lower] Andean Avocet. A bulky, large-headed avocet of the Andean salt lakes. Northern Chile, mid November.

[Upper left] Long-toed Lapwing. A jacana-like lapwing of African wetlands, it has long toes for a lapwing, but not as long as a jacana! Kenya, mid July.

[Lower left] Blacksmith Plover. Named for its call, which recalls a hammer striking an anvil. Cape Town, South Africa, mid November.

[Upper right] River Lapwing. The Indian equivalent of Spur-winged Lapwing, which it is often called in India. The shaggy crest is raised quite frequently. Uttar Pradesh, India, late December.

[Lower right] Black-headed Lapwing, nominate race. This species has tiny wattles at the base of the bill. A second race, *latifrons*, with more white on the forehead, occurs in the northeast of its range, in east Kenya and Somalia. Kenya, mid March.

Spur-winged Lapwing. A largely African lapwing, although some breed in the Near East and move south to winter in Africa. This is a north-bound migrant, passing through Cyprus. Late April.

[Upper left] Yellow-wattled Lapwing. A non-breeding adult. Breeding birds have a completely black crown and a blacker margin between the brown and white on the upper breast. Rajasthan, India, early January.

[Lower left] Senegal Lapwing. A misnomer if ever there was one – at the time of publication of the *Birds of Africa* in 1986 there was just one record of Senegal Lapwing in Senegal! Very similar to the slightly larger, but proportionally shorter legged (and also African) Black-winged Lapwing. The best field mark for adults (as is this bird) is the neat circular white forehead patch. Tanzania, mid July.

[Upper right] Crowned Lapwing. A widespread African species, from the Horn of Africa to the Cape. Adult. South Africa, mid November.

[Lower right] Black-winged Lapwing. The head pattern of adults of this species is more variable than with the similar Senegal Lapwing. Legs are dark red, black in Senegal Lapwing. Kenya, mid March.

[Upper left] Grey-headed Lapwing. This adult was breeding in arable farmland. Honshu, Japan, late April.

[Lower left] Red-wattled Lapwing. A south and south-eastern Asian species with three races, two of which can be distinguished in the field by the extent of white on the side of the neck. This is of the nominate race *indicus* and is a non-breeding adult with white flecking in the black of neck. Rajasthan, India, late December.

[Upper right] Banded Lapwing. An attractive grassland lapwing, endemic to Australia. New South Wales, Australia, late August.

[Lower right] African Wattled Lapwing. Another widespread African lapwing, with prominent yellow wattles. Johannesburg, South Africa, mid November.

[Right] Masked Lapwing. Race *miles* with less black on nape and shoulders but larger wattle than race *novaehollandiae* (see pages 74 and 169). Northern Territory, Australia, mid September.

[Middle] White-tailed Lapwing. A strongly migratory western Asian lapwing that occurs as a vagrant to Western Europe. Rajasthan, India, late December.

[Below] Andean Lapwing. A bird of high altitude grasslands. Northern Chile, mid November.

[Left] Red-kneed Dotterel. An atypical medium-sized plover, widespread on wetlands throughout Australia, the only member of genus *Erythrogonys*. Western Australia, late March.

[Middle] Inland Dotterel. A medium-sized plover of dry grasslands in Australia, with unusual face and breast patterns. New South Wales, Australia, late August.

[Below] Two Wrybills demonstrating their unique laterally/sideways curved bills. The total population is quite small, estimated as 5,100 birds in 1994. North Island, New Zealand, mid January.

European Golden Plover. An adult male on its moorland breeding grounds giving warning calls to his chicks. Iceland, late June.

[Opposite, upper right] Pacific Golden Plover. Adult moulting out of breeding plumage. Queensland, Australia, mid September.

[Lower right] American Golden Plover. In juvenile plumage, which is retained for some time by the *Pluvialis* group of plovers. Northern Chile, mid November.

24

Three lapwings are mainly Asian: River, Yellow-wattled and Red-wattled Lapwings. There are two South American species: the Southern Lapwing is widespread throughout South America and the Andean Lapwing is restricted to the Andes of Colombia, northern Argentina and Chile. Two species are found in Australasia: the Banded and Masked Lapwings. The Banded Lapwing is widespread in Australia away from the tropical north, and there are two races of Masked Lapwing, one of which (race *novaehollandiae*) colonised New Zealand naturally in the early 1930s, where it is now widespread.

ATYPICAL AND *PLUVIALIS* PLOVERS

The first group of small plovers consists of three Australasian species, all of different genera: Red-kneed Dotterel, Inland Dotterel and Wrybill. The Red-kneed Dotterel, as its name suggests, is a plover with red 'knees' and longish legs, widespread in Australia, while the Inland Dotterel is rather similar in size to the Eurasian Dotterel, although adults have striking black head and breast markings. The Wrybill is endemic to New Zealand and breeds on braided rivers in South Island. It is of particular interest as the only bird species – not just the only shorebird – that has an asymmetric bill, curved to the right, with which it feeds by probing and scraping.

There are four plover species in the *Pluvialis* group, all strongly migratory northern hemisphere species: three golden plovers – European, Pacific and American – and the Grey Plover, known in North America as Black-bellied Plover. The Grey Plover is one of the most widespread of all shorebirds, breeding throughout Arctic North America and Asia, migrating to winter coastally as far south as South America, southern Africa, southern Asia and Australasia.

CHARADRIUS AND OTHER SMALLER PLOVERS

There are 31 plovers in the genus *Charadrius*. The formerly widespread New Zealand Dotterel has declined to two widely separated subspecies, the largely sedentary race *obscurus* in the south and race *aquilonius* on North Island. The population of *obscurus* is tiny in spite of considerable investment in predator control; that of

[Above] New Zealand Dotterel. The nominate race *obscurus* breeds on open moorland on Stewart Island, off South Island, in very similar habitat to that used by Eurasian Dotterel. A feature of this race is the pale area around the eye; compare with race *aquilonius* that breeds in North Island (page 154). Stewart Island, New Zealand, late November.

[Upper right] Semipalmated Plover. This photo shows the palmation between the inner toes, a feature of this species, but not shown by the closely related and very similar Common Ringed Plover. The black head markings show this to be a male. Florida, USA, late May.

[Lower right] Long-billed Plover. A sparsely distributed small to medium-sized Asian plover of rather pebbly areas, such as this stream bed. South Korea, early May.

aquilonius is estimated to be about 1,400 birds. Then there is a group of seven smaller 'ringed' plover species, although not all are ringed in that some do not have a complete dark breast-band. They have a northern hemisphere distribution: the Common Ringed and Little Ringed in Europe and Asia, Long-billed in east Asia, and the other four (Semipalmated, Wilson's, Killdeer and Piping Plover) in North America or northern South America. Most are migratory or have migratory races. The migratory races of both Common Ringed and Little Ringed Plover have distinct non-breeding plumages in which the black in the head pattern and breast-band is largely lost, becoming brown, whilst the sedentary races of both species moult more-or-less directly from one breeding plumage to the next. Bill patterns and colours, however, are only developed fully when breeding.

Of six small African plovers, three are very similar and are obviously closely related: Madagascan, Kittlitz's and St Helena Plovers. Kittlitz's is widespread in Africa and seems to be the ancestral form of the other two – the St Helena Plover, which occurs on St Helena in the south Atlantic, and the Madagascan Plover, which is found on Madagascar where Kittlitz's Plover also occurs. The other three are Three-banded, Forbes's and White-fronted Plovers. Three-banded and Forbes's Plovers are similar and also closely related; the former largely occurring south of the equator, whilst Forbes's is found in equatorial West and central Africa. The White-fronted Plover is quite plain, with a white forehead and a rufous-tinged breast when breeding, and occurs in Africa mainly south of the equator and also in Madagascar.

The Kentish Plover of Europe and Asia, Snowy Plover of North America and also Javan Plover were, until recently, regarded as races of Kentish Plover. The first two are widespread in their respective continents, where the more northerly populations are migratory, whilst the Javan Plover is sedentary and restricted to Java, Indonesia. Adults of all three are visually very similar, with a white hind-neck collar and small breast-side patches, differing mainly in the presence or absence of black between eye and bill, and the extent of rufous on the head.

Another widely distributed grouping of small plovers is Red-capped (Australia), Malaysian (Southeast Asia), Chestnut-banded

27

[Opposite page, upper left] Little Ringed Plover. Breeding male, race *curonicus*. The very black head markings indicate a male. South Korea, early May.

[Opposite page, upper right] Piping Plover. A small, pale, stubby billed plover of North and Central America. Florida, USA, mid May.

[Opposite page, lower left] Killdeer. Named for its call, "kill-deee". Adult non-breeding. California, USA, early November.

[Opposite page, lower right] Madagascan Plover. This species is endemic to Madagascar; it has presumably evolved from Kittlitz's Plover, which is widespread both in Africa and in Madagascar, and with which it shares its head pattern, although not the black breast band. A male. Madagascar, late November.

[Right] Kittlitz's Plover. A small plover widespread throughout much of sub-Saharan Africa. South Africa, early November.

[Middle] Three-banded Plover. Another widespread small African plover. South Africa, mid November.

[Below] White-fronted Plover. A pale, relatively poorly marked small African plover. South Africa, early November.

Kentish Plover. A small plover of Europe and Asia, with small breast-side patches, not a breast-band. Breeding male. The black areas become browner when not breeding, similar to the closely related Snowy Plover (see next image). Cyprus, late April.

[Upper left] Snowy Plover. The North American equivalent of Kentish Plover. Non-breeding adult. California, USA, early November.

[Lower left] Chestnut-banded Plover. A small African ringed plover with a chestnut-brown breast-band. South Africa, early November.

[Upper right] Malaysian Plover. Similar to Kentish Plover, but always has larger breast-side patches and often has a complete, but narrow, breast-band. Thailand, late November.

[Lower right] Red-capped Plover. The Australian equivalent of Kentish and Snowy Plovers of Eurasia and America, respectively. Queensland, Australia, mid September.

31

[Upper left] Puna Plover. A small plover of Andean saline wetlands. As with other similar plovers, the black on the head (rather than brown-black) indicates a male. Northern Chile, mid November.

[Lower left] Two-banded Plover. A small- to medium-sized plover of South America. The population on the Falkland Islands often has the upper breast-band reduced to side patches. Adult breeding, probably a male. Southern Argentina, late November.

[Upper right] Collared Plover. A small ringed plover of Central and South America. Venezuela, mid November.

[Lower right] Greater Sand Plover. Of the western race *columbinus*, which is less strongly marked than the eastern races. Cyprus, late April.

(southern Africa), Collared (Central and South America), Puna (Andes, South America), Two-banded (Southern South America) and Double-banded (Australasia) Plovers. The first five are in many respects similar in size and general behaviour to Kentish and Snowy Plovers, but they are sedentary or make relatively short seasonal or altitudinal movements when not breeding. The other two, as their names suggest, both have two breast-bands in breeding plumage, both bands black in Two-banded (although birds in the Falkland Islands often have a broken upper band), whilst the upper band is black and the lower rufous in Double-banded Plover. Some Two-banded Plovers move short distances north when not breeding, but the Double-banded Plover is one of very few shorebird species that has a long-distance migration entirely within the southern hemisphere, with many of the birds breeding in South Island, New Zealand, moving to Australia in the Austral winter.

There are several races of both Lesser and Greater Sand Plovers, all migratory. The Lesser Sand Plover breeds in a number of discreet areas in central and eastern Asia, and winters coastally in southern and eastern Africa, through the Middle East, south Asia to Australia. The breeding range of the Greater Sand Plover is similarly confined to Asia, although its breeding distribution is more westerly and its wintering range extends further west to northern Africa.

A group of five closely related medium-sized plovers is formed by the Caspian Plover, Oriental Plover, Eurasian Dotterel, Rufous-chested Plover and Mountain Plover. They are all migratory, although some more so than others. The very similar Caspian and Oriental Plovers are a 'species pair' – Caspian Plovers breed in western Central Asia and wintering in eastern and southern Africa, whilst Oriental Plovers breed in northern China and Mongolia, probably flying non-stop to and from north-western Australia on both annual migrations. The Eurasian Dotterel's breeding distribution ranges from Scotland to far eastern Siberia, and also in an isolated area in central Asia. They have reversed sexual roles, with the female being the brighter, reflecting their serial polyandrous mating system (see Chapter 5). They winter in semi-desert areas in North Africa, and so the east Siberian breeders have a long north-

[Upper] Lesser Sand Plover, race *stegmanni* (from the north-eastern portion of the breeding range). Adult in breeding plumage, on northbound migration. South Korea, late April.

[Lower] Eurasian Dotterel. A juvenile on migration that will probably winter in North Africa. Note the pale, crescentic breast-band that is more prominent on adults. Cornwall, UK, mid September.

[Upper left] Rufous-chested Dotterel. Breeding male; has slightly more black in the head pattern and a brighter red breast than the female. Southern Chile, late November.

[Lower left] Caspian Plover. An adult moulting to non-breeding plumage. Kenya, early September.

[Opposite, right] Mountain Plover. The North American equivalent of Eurasian Dotterel. Adult. Colorado, USA, mid April.

[Opposite, middle] Hooded Plover. One of the two species of *Thinornis* plovers, the other being Shore Plover (see page 197). The south-eastern Australian race *cucullatus*. Victoria, Australia, early September.

[Opposite, below] Black-fronted Dotterel. A striking small Australasian plover, the only member of its genus *Elseyornis*. Northern Territory, Australia, mid September.

east to south-west migration. The Rufous-chested Plover, a South American species, breeds in southern Chile, southern Argentina and the Falkland Islands. Part of the population is sedentary, whilst others, including the Falkland's birds, migrate north in the Austral winter. The Mountain Plover, a declining species due to loss of breeding habitat, breeds in central USA and winters from California to south-east Texas.

There are two *Thinornis* plover species, both of which are small: Hooded Plover of Australia and Shore Plover of New Zealand. The Hooded Plover is a sedentary coastal plover of sandy beaches. There are two distinctive races: nominate race *cucullatus* in south-east Australia and *tregallasi* in southern Western Australia. The Shore Plover is endemic to New Zealand, with a tiny population estimated in 2016 to be little more than 60 birds. Probably originally widespread in New Zealand, by the late 1800s the natural wild population was restricted to the predator-free Chatham Islands. Captive-reared birds have been released on several New Zealand inshore islands, but with little success (see Chapter 5).

The final five plovers (Black-fronted and Tawny-throated Dotterels, Diademed Sandpiper-plover, Pied Plover and Egyptian Plover) are a rather disparate group, all of different genera. Black-fronted Dotterel is a freshwater, sedentary species, occurring throughout Australia and to a lesser extent New Zealand, which it colonised from the 1950s. Tawny-throated Dotterel is a South American species mainly occurring west of the Andes, from northern Peru to south Chile. Diademed Sandpiper-plover is a small largely sedentary plover of the high Andes, distributed from northern Peru south to central Chile. It has a longish, slightly decurved bill reminiscent of a *Calidris* species that has led to the 'Sandpiper-plover' element of its name. Pied Plover, a sedentary species of north and central South America, although smaller than the lapwings is very lapwing-like, and hence its alternative English name 'Pied Lapwing'. The last of this group is Egyptian Plover, a shorebird of tropical west to central Africa, formerly thought to be a courser or pratincole, now placed in its own family.

[Right] Tawny-throated Dotterel. A medium-sized plover of western and southern South America. Southern Chile, late November.

[Middle] Diademed Sandpiper-plover. An iconic small plover of the Andes. Northern Chile, late November.

[Below] Pied Plover. A lapwing-like medium-sized plover. Venezuela, mid November.

[Upper left] Greater Painted-snipe. Widespread in the hotter areas of Africa and Asia. An immature female. Rajasthan, India, late December.

[Lower left] Madagascan Jacana. Showing its neck pattern that is the reverse of African Jacana. Madagascar, early December.

[Upper right] African Jacana. In this species the hind-neck is dark and the fore-neck off-white, curiously the reverse of the neck-pattern of the closely related Madagascan Jacana. Kenya, mid March.

[Lower right] Comb-crested Jacana. Jacanas truly deserve their popular name of 'lily-trotters' because their extraordinarily long toes and claws allow them to spread their weight as they walk (and also nest) on water-lily leaves. Northern Territory, Australia, mid September.

[Upper] Pheasant-tailed Jacana. Unusually for a jacana, this species has both a breeding and a non-breeding plumage; this is the latter. Rajasthan, India, early January.

[Lower] Bronze-winged Jacana. Rajasthan, India, early January.

PAINTED-SNIPES AND JACANAS

There are three species of painted-snipe: Greater Painted-snipe in southern, south-eastern and eastern Asia; the closely related Australian Painted-snipe, relatively recently split from Greater; and the South American Painted-snipe of south-central South America. Painted-snipes are perhaps best described as nomadic, moving in relation to changing wetland conditions. They are more closely related to the jacanas than to the true snipes and, reflecting their polyandrous breeding system (see Chapter 5), the female is larger, with brighter plumage than the male.

There are eight species of jacana in six genera, all found in the tropics. The popular name for jacanas – 'lily-trotters' – describes them well because all have extremely long toes that allow them to walk on floating vegetation, particularly water-lily leaves. African and Madagascan Jacanas are closely related, as are Northern and Wattled Jacanas of Central and South America. All the other species are monotypic: Comb-crested Jacana of tropical Australia, and Pheasant-tailed and Bronze-winged Jacanas, both of southern and south-eastern Asia. Pheasant-tailed Jacanas in the northern part of their range are the only truly migratory jacanas; however, as with painted snipe, all jacanas will move if their wetlands dry out. The Pheasant-tailed is also the only jacana to have a distinct breeding plumage – when it acquires the long tail that gives it its name. The Lesser Jacana is an African species that has a juvenile-type plumage pattern year-round and is by far the smallest species. As with some lapwings, a few of the jacanas have sharp carpal spurs at the bend of the wing that are used largely in display (see Chapter 4).

Wattled Jacana. A Capybara *Hydrochoerus hydrochaeris*, the world's largest rodent, provides a look-out perch for both a Cattle Tyrant *Machetornis rixosus* (left) and a Wattled Jacana. Venezuela, mid November.

PLAINS-WANDERER AND SEEDSNIPES

The Plains-wanderer, endemic to eastern Australia, is the sole member of the *Pedionomidae*. Formerly placed with the buttonquails, which it resembles superficially, it has been recognised as a true shorebird since the 1980s. Juvenile and adult male are similar, but the females are slightly larger and brighter than the males, consistent with their presumed serial polyandrous breeding strategy. Largely sedentary, it makes significant but random movements in response to rains or dry periods. The population of the Plains-wanderer is declining due to loss of its native sparse grassland habitat.

The nearest relatives of the Plains-wanderer are the four South American seedsnipes of the Andes and Patagonia: the rather larger Rufous-bellied and White-bellied Seedsnipes of genus *Attagis*, and the smaller Grey-breasted and Least Seedsnipes of genus *Thinocorus*. They superficially resemble small game birds, but when they fly their long slender wings confirm their shorebird status. It is possible that both Plains-wanderer and the four seedsnipes have the same unusual primary moult sequence, in which the three outer primaries are moulted before a complex sequence of the inner primaries, perhaps consistent with their common relationship.

[Upper] Plains-wanderer. Endemic to Australia, it is probably most closely related to the South American Seedsnipes. Female, larger and more colourful than the male, reflecting its possible serial polyandrous breeding system. Australia, late August.

[Lower] Rufous-bellied Seedsnipe. Males, as this probably is, are darker below with more extensive patterning on the lower breast than females. Chile, mid November.

White-bellied Seedsnipe. This bird has two chicks.
Tierra del Fuego, Argentina, early December.

[Upper left] Grey-breasted Seedsnipe. A female demonstrating her cryptic plumage (see page 199, for a male). Chile, mid November.

[Lower left] Least Seedsnipe. A male, nominate race *rumicivorus*. Southern Chile, late November.

[Opposite, right] Eurasian Woodcock. The wintering population of Eurasian Woodcocks in western Europe is much larger than in the breeding season. Northamptonshire, UK, late January.

[Opposite, middle] Jack Snipe. A very secretive species, that only flies when almost trodden on! Norfolk, UK, early November.

[Opposite, below] Latham's Snipe. Breeds in Japan and far-eastern Russia, and winters in south-east Australia. Juvenile. Queensland, Australia, early September

WOODCOCKS AND THE TRUE SNIPES

Of the eight woodcock species, the Eurasian Woodcock is by far the most numerous and widespread, breeding from western Europe to eastern Asia. When they are not breeding, they move south to spend the winter in northern and central Africa to south-eastern Asia. There are six largely sedentary species in the Far East, each apparently restricted to a single island: Amami, Javan, New Guinea, Burkidnon, Sulawesi and Moluccan Woodcocks. The only other widespread species is American Woodcock, which breeds in eastern USA and southern Canada, and winters in southern USA.

There are 21 species of snipe in three genera: *Coenocorypha*, *Lymnocryptes* and *Gallinago*. The *Coenocorypha* snipe are three small sedentary species that are confined to isolated New Zealand islands and were formerly lumped as Subantarctic Snipe, but are now split, adding Chatham and Snares Snipes. The sole representative of the second genus *Lymnocryptes* is Jack Snipe, another small snipe ('Jack' means small), which has a distribution from northern Europe to central Siberia and that winters south to Africa and south Asia.

The remaining 17 species of *Gallinago* snipe are distributed worldwide. Some are strongly migratory; others simply move altitudinally – and many are sedentary. Solitary Snipe is a widespread Asian species, some of which migrate south through central Asia and India, but others are merely altitudinal migrants. Latham's and Great Snipe are strongly migratory. Latham's Snipe breeds in parts of the Russian Far East and Japan, moving south to winter in eastern Australia, whilst Great Snipe breeds in northern Scandinavia and west Russia, and migrates to Africa (see Chapter 6).

Wood Snipe is a sedentary or altitudinal migrant of south and south-east Asia. Pin-tailed Snipe breeds over a broad area of boreal Siberia, with western birds migrating south over the Himalayas, and eastern birds through east Asia. Swinhoe's Snipe breeds in central and southern Siberia, with a non-breeding range that extends from India to New Guinea and northern Australia. African and Madagascan Snipe are both sedentary.

The two subspecies of Common Snipe, *gallinago* and *faroeensis*, are not separable in the field. The former is widespread from western

[Above] South American Snipe, another species very similar to Common Snipe. Southern Chile, late November.

[Opposite, right] Great Snipe. Identified by the band of white-tipped wing-coverts. Kenya, mid September.

[Opposite, middle] Wilson's Snipe. Very similar to Common Snipe, but darker above and with darker flank barring. Adult. Colorado, USA, late April.

[Opposite, below] Asian Dowitchers. A group about to migrate north to their breeding grounds. Western Australia, early April.

Europe through Asia to eastern Siberia, wintering south to Africa, and also south and south-east Asia, whilst the latter breeds in Iceland, Faeroes, Orkney and Shetlands, and winters in Britain and Ireland. Wilson's Snipe of North America is very similar to Common Snipe, but can be distinguished by its slightly different flight pattern, its strongly barred underwing and its display flight, in which it fans its outer two tail feathers, not just the single outer-most, as does the Common Snipe (see page 201). Breeding throughout North America, Wilson's Snipe winters in southern USA, Central and northern South America.

All the poorly known South American snipe (South American, Puna, Noble, Giant, Fuegian, Jameson's and Imperial Snipe) are largely sedentary.

DOWITCHERS, GODWITS AND CURLEWS

The three dowitcher species *Limnodromus* form a link between the snipes and the godwits. They share with the snipe their long, straight bills, their sewing-machine-like deep probing feeding style, and their rather similar, though longer-legged structure. They also resemble the godwits because they have distinctive rufous breeding plumages. The North American Short-billed Dowitcher has three races that are identifiable in breeding plumage, although the Long-billed Dowitcher (north America and neighbouring Siberia) and Asian Dowitcher (central and eastern Asia) are both monotypic. All three species are migratory, with Asian perhaps moving the greatest distances, as far south as Australia, although their main wintering area is probably south Sumatra, Indonesia.

There are four godwits worldwide, all breeding in the northern hemisphere: Black-tailed, Hudsonian, Bar-tailed and Marbled Godwits. Black-tailed and Bar-tailed breed in Europe and Asia, Hudsonian and Marbled Godwits in North America. There are three subspecies of Black-tailed Godwit: *islandica* that breeds in Iceland and winters through Britain and Ireland to the Iberian Peninsula; *limosa* breeding from western Europe to central Asia; and *melanuroides*, which breeds in eastern Siberia and winters in south-eastern Asia and Australia. The Yellow Sea is used as a stop-over site by about 50,000 birds of the latter race during both north and southbound migration.

Hudsonian Godwits. Moulting to non-breeding plumage. Northern Chile, mid November.

Black-tailed Godwits. Race *islandica*, leaving a high
tide roost. Norfolk, UK, mid April.

There are a number of subspecies of Bar-tailed Godwits, which between them breed from northern Scandinavia in Europe, across northern Asia to western Alaska in the east. For identification, three racial groups can be recognised, depending on the extent of white on the back when seen in flight: (1) *lapponica* with *taymyrensis*, (2) *menzbieri* and (3) *baueri*. All are coastal when not breeding, with *lapponica* and *taymyrensis* moving as far south as coastal South Africa, *menzbieri* migrating mainly to northern Western Australia and south-eastern Asia, and *baueri* wintering in New Zealand and eastern Australia.

Hudsonian Godwit is a particularly long-distance migrant, breeding in Arctic Canada and wintering in southern South America, while Marbled Godwit breeds in central Canada and USA and winters in southern USA and Central America.

The IOC list includes nine species of curlew (Little Curlew; Eskimo Curlew; Whimbrel; Bristle-thighed Curlew; Slender-billed Curlew; Eurasian Curlew; Far Eastern Curlew and Long-billed Curlew), together with Upland Sandpiper, the only representative of its genus *Bartramia*. It seems most likely that the Eskimo Curlew is extinct and there have also not been any reliable reports of Slender-billed Curlew since 2001, so that species may also be extinct.

The Little Curlew breeds in Siberia, with most of its population migrating to northern Australia in the northern winter, the exact wintering location depending upon the variable extent of dry grasslands and freshwater wetlands which may vary greatly between years. Whimbrels are one of the most widespread shorebirds, breeding worldwide, although discontinuously in the Arctic, and with a wintering distribution that includes Africa, central and south-eastern Asia, Australasia and the Americas. The different races of Whimbrel may be separated into four groups for identification: (1) *phaeopus* with *islandicus*, which have a white rump and back; (2) *alboaxillaris* with white, unbarred underwings; (3) *variegatus*, which has a white rump only; and (4) the North American race, 'Hudsonian' Whimbrel, which differs from the Eurasian races in being darker and more contrasting above, particularly in the head pattern, and more buffish, less white below, and shows an entirely brown back in flight.

[Above] Marsh Sandpiper. In fresh
breeding plumage. Cyprus, early April.

[Opposite, left] Far Eastern Curlew. This species has
uniformly brown upperparts, lacking the white back
of Eurasian Curlew. South Korea, late April.

[Opposite, middle] Long-billed Curlew.
The longest billed shorebird. Acquiring its
breeding plumage. Florida, USA, early April.

[Opposite, below] Upland Sandpiper. An atypical, short-
billed curlew of the North American prairie grasslands
that winters in South America. Kansas, USA, late April.

Bristle-thighed Curlew breeds in Alaska and winters in the Pacific; it shares with African (and perhaps Madagascan) Jacana the distinction of being the only shorebirds to become flightless during their wing-moult (see Chapter 2).

The widespread and relatively numerous Eurasian Curlew breeds from Europe westward to central Asia and Kazakhstan and, depending on race, may either be locally sedentary or migrate south to Africa and southern and south-eastern Asia. The races differ mainly in the extent of underwing barring. Far Eastern Curlew breeds in eastern Russia and north-eastern China and is a long-distance migrant to Australia, often flying there directly. Long-billed Curlew of North America is, on average, the longest billed of all shorebirds – it breeds in the mid-west USA and winters coastally in southern USA and Central America. The Upland Sandpiper is a small, short-billed curlew breeding in the prairies of central North America and wintering in South American grasslands.

THE *TRINGA* AND RELATED SANDPIPERS

There are 13 species in the genus *Tringa*, all of which breed in the northern hemisphere and are migratory. Spotted Redshank breeds from northern Europe to eastern Russia, and throughout the year it uses inland wetlands, wintering from south-western Europe and Africa to south-eastern Asia. The closely related Common Redshank has a more southerly breeding distribution, from western Europe to central Asia. The southerly breeders are relatively sedentary, whilst the more northerly birds migrate to northern Africa and southern and south-eastern Asia. Although there are a number of races, none can be separated in the field. The Marsh Sandpiper breeds from eastern Europe to central Asia, wintering in southern Africa, south and south-west Asia, and Australia. The Common Greenshank has a broad breeding distribution from western Europe to eastern Russia, and an equally widespread, low density, freshwater non-breeding distribution from Africa to Australasia.

The endangered Nordmann's Greenshank breeds in far-eastern Russia and winters mainly in Bangladesh and south-eastern Asia, migrating through the Yellow Sea area. Greater and Lesser Yellowlegs, which are the North American equivalents of Common

[Opposite] Spotted Redshank. A male in fresh breeding plumage on its northbound migration. South Korea, early May.

[Upper left] Nordmann's Greenshanks. An endangered species with a population probably less than 1,000 birds. These two are both acquiring breeding plumage. South Korea, early May.

[Lower left] Lesser Yellowlegs. Moulting into breeding plumage. Florida, mid March.

[Upper right] Greater Yellowlegs. An adult moulting to non-breeding plumage, just completing wing moult, its outer primaries still growing. Florida, USA, late October.

[Lower right] Solitary Sandpiper. Moulting to first non-breeding plumage. Venezuela, mid November.

[Right] Wood Sandpiper. Juvenile. Norfolk, UK, mid August.

[Middle] Grey-tailed Tattler. Adult in breeding plumage. Wandering Tattler in breeding plumage have more extensive, darker barring on the underparts. South Korea, mid May.

[Below] Wandering Tattler. Non-breeding adult. Note the greater extension of the primaries beyond the tail than with Grey-tailed Tattler. California, USA, mid November.

Greenshank and Common Redshank, respectively, both breed in northern North America and winter from southern USA and throughout South America. Of the smaller *Tringa*, Green Sandpiper has a broad breeding distribution across northern Europe and Asia and a wintering range that does not extend very far south of the equator, from Africa to south-eastern Asia. Its North American equivalent is the very similar Solitary Sandpiper, which, although it breeds at similar latitudes to Green Sandpiper, winters in South America to well south of the equator. Wood Sandpiper, the smallest *Tringa*, is widespread throughout Europe and Asia, and breeds from western Europe to eastern Russia, migrating to Africa, southern and south-eastern Asia, and Australia.

The two tattler species are medium sized: Grey-tailed Tattler breeds in eastern Siberia with most of the population wintering in northern Australia, and the very similar Wandering Tattler breeds in North America and migrates to the Pacific islands east of Australasia. There are two races of Willet, the largest of the *Tringa* species, which has a striking black-and-white wing pattern, unexpected until it flies. There are two races: the 'Western' Willet breeds in central Canada and USA and winters in southern USA and the Caribbean, and the 'Eastern' Willet breeds in eastern USA and winters as far south as northern South America. Western Willets average 15% larger than Eastern Willets.

Willet. Second calendar-year birds, both retaining a few juvenile feathers. Florida, late March.

TEREK SANDPIPER, *ACTITIS* SANDPIPERS AND TURNSTONES

The Terek Sandpiper, which apart from its upturned bill, recalls a small *Tringa* species, has an extensive breeding distribution from eastern Europe to eastern Russia and an equally extensive coastal winter distribution in the southern hemisphere, from west Africa to eastern Australia. Common Sandpiper, as a breeding species, is distributed from western Europe to eastern Siberia and winters widely throughout much of Africa, southern and south-eastern Asia, as far as Australia. Spotted Sandpiper is the North American equivalent of the Common Sandpiper, distinguished by its spotted underparts in breeding plumage. It breeds widely in northern North America and winters in southern USA, Central and much of South America. The Tuamotu Sandpiper is a small, endangered shorebird

that is restricted to a small group of islands in the central Pacific. It is the only remaining representative of a Pacific island genus, several species of which have been wiped out by the introduction of rats and other predators.

There are two races of Ruddy Turnstone: *interpres* which is found in Europe, Africa and Asia, and *morinella* in the Americas. They occur coastally year-round and are consequently one of the most widespread of all shorebirds. A second turnstone species, Black Turnstone, occurs only on the rocky Pacific coast of North America, breeding in Alaska and wintering from southern Canada south to Mexico. As the name turnstone suggests, both species frequently feed by turning stones, seaweed and other debris with their bills as they search for food.

CALIDRIS AND RELATED SANDPIPERS

Although not a *Calidris* species, Surfbird nonetheless appears to be closely related to that genus. It breeds inland in Alaska and, when not breeding, it occurs on the rocky shores of the Pacific coasts of both North and South America.

There are 19 species in the genus *Calidris*, all breeding in the northern hemisphere and all migratory to a greater or lesser extent. Great Knot, the largest *Calidris*, is restricted to the East Asia and Australasia Flyway (see Chapter 6). Its northern Australian wintering grounds were only discovered in the early 1980s, and as a result the estimate of its world population was revised almost overnight from 5,000 to 500,000! It breeds in eastern Siberia and winters in Southeast Asia, as well as Australia. The Red Knot has a scattered breeding distribution throughout the Arctic, and winters coastally from western Europe, Africa, the Far East, Australasia and southern USA to the far south of South America. No less than six subspecies are recognised, a consequence of its scattered breeding distribution. Sanderling breeds in the high Arctic and is another widespread shorebird in both hemispheres, particularly in the non-breeding season.

The following nine *Calidris* species are a group of fairly similar small sandpipers, often referred to as 'peeps' in North America. Among them are five North American Arctic breeding

[Opposite, upper left] Spotted Sandpiper. Adult in non-breeding plumage. Some still retain a few breeding plumage underpart spots at this time. Florida, USA, mid October.

[Opposite, lower left] Terek Sandpiper. Adult in breeding plumage about to pick up a food item. Note the palmate feet (see Chapter 4). South Korea, early May.

[Above] Ruddy Turnstones. A small group, all in non-breeding plumage. As they are a high Arctic species they breed relatively late, and therefore show little or no breeding plumage at this time. Gwynedd, UK, early April.

[Above] Great Knots. Five birds in breeding plumage at their Yellow Sea stopover site, about to depart on the final leg of their northbound migration. The convex undertail is where the fuel for migration is stored! South Korea, late May.

[Opposite, upper left] Semipalmated Sandpiper. A juvenile, showing a palmate foot. Florida, USA, mid September.

[Opposite, upper right] Western Sandpiper. A breeding adult, also showing its palmate feet. Florida, mid May.

[Opposite, lower left] Red-necked Stint. A breeding adult, on migration, Yellow Sea, South Korea, early May.

[Opposite, lower right] Little Stint. Adult acquiring breeding plumage. Cyprus, early May.

[Upper left] Long-toed Stint. One of the three yellow-legged stints (the others are Temminck's Stint and Least Sandpiper). It is well named – the middle toe is diagnostically longer than the tarsus. Non-breeding plumage. Western Australia, late March.

[Upper right] Least Sandpiper. A non-breeding bird showing its yellow legs. California, USA, early November.

[Lower left] White-rumped Sandpiper. First non-breeding on its wintering grounds. Note the contrast between the fresh upperparts and the faded, pale fringed juvenile wing-coverts. Argentina, late November.

[Lower right] Baird's Sandpiper. Non-breeding. Tierra del Fuego, Argentina, early December.

species: Semipalmated, Western, Least, White-rumped and Baird's Sandpipers. Little and Temminck's Stints breed in Arctic Europe and Asia, while Red-necked and Long-toed Stints breed in Arctic Asia and central Asia respectively. Their wintering areas largely reflect their breeding distributions: Semipalmated Sandpiper is found coastally in South America; Western and Least Sandpipers coastally in southern USA, Central America and northern South America; and both White-rumped and Baird's Sandpipers winter in southern South America. The Little Stint is widespread in Africa, Temminck's Stint occurs from central Africa to India and Southeast Asia, and the Red-necked Stint and Long-toed Stint from Southeast Asia to Australia. The majority of the population of Red-necked Stints winter in Australia.

Pectoral Sandpiper, which breeds in high Arctic Siberia and Canada, is one of three quite closely related species, the other two being the very similar Sharp-tailed Sandpiper and Curlew Sandpiper. Pectoral Sandpiper occasionally interbreeds with Curlew Sandpiper, resulting in the hybrid 'Cox's Sandpiper'. Both Sharp-tailed and Curlew Sandpipers breed in northern Siberia, but not in North America. Most Pectoral Sandpipers winter in southern South America, although a few are regularly seen in Southeast Australia and in New Zealand, and Sharp-tailed Sandpipers winter in Southeast Asia and Australasia. In winter, Curlew Sandpipers are distributed from west Africa, eastwards to Southeast Asia and Australia.

The four remaining *Calidris* species are Purple Sandpiper of the north Atlantic, Rock Sandpiper of the north Pacific, Dunlin which has a circumpolar breeding distribution, and Stilt Sandpiper which breeds in northern Canada. Neither Purple nor Rock Sandpiper move very far south in winter, so that the more northerly birds of these two species probably winter as far north as any species of shorebird. Dunlins move south in winter but do not reach the equator, and although a few Stilt Sandpipers winter in southern USA, the majority move south of the equator to central South America.

The last shorebirds in this group can best be described as 'near-Calidrids': Spoon-billed, Broad-billed and Buff-breasted

[Upper left] Sharp-tailed Sandpiper. First non-breeding. North Island, New Zealand, mid November.

[Lower left] Curlew Sandpiper. First non-breeding. This plumage is only acquired once they have reached the wintering area, and is not seen in Europe. South Africa, early November.

[Opposite, right] Purple Sandpiper. Adult breeding, on the breeding grounds. Iceland, late June.

[Opposite, middle] Stilt Sandpiper. Non-breeding. Florida, USA, late March.

[Opposite, below] Broad-billed Sandpiper. Holding a food item. Adult, non-breeding. Thailand, mid November.

Sandpipers, and Ruff. The Spoon-billed Sandpiper is one of the world's most threatened shorebirds, with a small breeding population on the Chukotski Peninsula of eastern Russia and winters from south-eastern India to south-eastern Asia. Broad-billed Sandpiper breeds in northern Europe and central Siberia, and winters from eastern Africa to Australia. Buff-breasted Sandpiper breeds from northeast Siberia to northern Canada, wintering in the pampas of central South America, but juveniles are annual in small numbers in western Europe, making it tempting to wonder if a small population may winter in Africa. The final 'near-Calidrid' is the Ruff, which has been described as 'the most interesting bird in the world' on the strength of its range of plumages, particularly those of breeding males, no two of which are ever exactly the same, and which are well known for their lekking breeding strategy. They breed from northern Europe to far-eastern Siberia and winter primarily in Africa, but with small numbers eastward to India.

PHALAROPES, COURSERS AND PRATINCOLES

There are three species of phalarope, all small or medium-sized, and all breeding in the northern hemisphere: Wilson's Phalarope breeds in North America, while Red-necked and Grey ('Red' in North America) Phalaropes have circumpolar breeding distributions. Wilson's Phalarope winters on South American wetlands, but both the other species winter in the open ocean, the only shorebirds to do so – Red-necked Phalarope in the Arabian Gulf, in the Pacific off South America and north of New Guinea, and Grey Phalarope in the Pacific off South America and in the Atlantic off West and South Africa.

Coursers are distinctive slender, small-headed and long-necked shorebirds of hot climates that use arid open or lightly wooded habitats. They have short, slightly decurved bills and often prefer to run rather than fly. In the case of the five *Cursorius* coursers (Cream-coloured, Somali, Burchell's, Temminck's, Indian), they have long off-white legs. The four *Rhinoptilus* coursers (Double-banded, Three-banded, Bronze-winged and Jerdon's) are larger and differ from *Cursorius* coursers in having a more patterned head, neck and breast, white uppertail-coverts (Indian Courser is the only *Cursorius* courser

[Right] Buff-breasted Sandpiper. First non-breeding, a plumage only infrequently seen in either North America and Europe. The tips of the juvenile wing-coverts have dark spots, while the upperparts are broad buff-fringed adult-type feathers. Juveniles have smaller, very dark upperpart feather with neat, narrow pale fringes. Thought to be the second record for Chile; they usually winter east of the Andes. Northern Chile, mid November.

[Middle] Ruffs, both juveniles, male (behind) and female. Juvenile Ruffs have individually variable plumage patterns; here the male's upperpart feathers show more detail, but the female is darker. Cornwall, UK, early September.

[Below] Red-necked Phalarope. Breeding female. Iceland, late June.

Pair of Grey/Red Phalaropes. Note the lobed and palmate feet of the more brightly coloured female, left. Iceland, late June.

[Upper left] Cream-coloured Courser.
Adult on migration. Cyprus, early May.

[Lower left] Australian Pratincole. A rather long-legged, courser-
like pratincole. Northern Territory, Australia, mid September.

[Upper right] Somali Courser. Kenya, mid September.

[Lower right] Oriental Pratincole. This eastern Asian
breeding species sometimes winters in Australia in
vast numbers. Western Australia, late March.

to have white uppertail-coverts), more variably coloured legs and large eyes indicative of their generally nocturnal behaviour. All are African, apart from Indian and Jerdon's Coursers of India, and all are sedentary or largely so, apart from Cream-coloured Courser whose populations breeding in North Africa and the Middle East are migratory.

The final group of shorebirds – pratincoles – are medium-sized with short bills, short legs and forked tails that, like swallows, specialise in aerial foraging for insects. All have white rumps. They are widely distributed in the old world tropics, from southern Europe, Africa, south and south-east Asia to Australia. Although they usually feed on the wing, they may also forage on the ground with a rather plover-like stand–watch–run technique. They generally breed in loose colonies and occur in flocks outside the breeding season. There are eight species, of which five are largely African: Collared, Black-winged, Madagascan, Rock and Grey Pratincoles. Two are found in south and south-east Asia: the Oriental and Small Pratincole. The eighth species is the long-legged Australian Pratincole, the only member of the genus *Stiltia* and which in many ways is a link between the coursers and the other pratincoles, which are all members of the genus *Glareola*. The Australian Pratincole, as its name suggests, breeds in Australia, and some migrate north after breeding to Papua New Guinea, Timor and Indonesia. Some African species are also migratory, notably Collared and Black-winged, both of which breed in Europe and Asia and winter in Africa, whilst the Madagascan breeds in Madagascar but moves to East Africa after breeding (see Chapter 6). The other African species are largely sedentary or make random weather-related movements. Oriental Pratincoles (which breed in north-eastern Asia) are migratory and move to northern Australia. An extraordinary count of 2.88 million Oriental Pratincoles in north-western Australia in February 2004 was perhaps the result of weather conditions forcing them to concentrate in one area.

[Upper] Rock Pratincole. Namibia, late December.

[Lower] Collared Pratincole. A widespread European, Asian and African species. Cyprus, early April.

REFERENCES

Aikman, H. and Miskelly, C., 2004. *Birds of the Chatham Islands.* New Zealand Department of Conservation.

Bamford, M.J., 1990. RAOU Survey of migratory waders in Kakadu National Park: Phase III. Report to the Australian National Parks and Wildlife Services. RAOU Report No. 7.

Banks, J.C. and Patterson, A.M., 2007. A preliminary study of the genetic differences in New Zealand oystercatcher species. *New Zealand Journal of Zoology* **34**, 141–144.

Barter, M.A., 2002. BirdLife International 2016. Species factsheet: Great Knot *Calidris tenuirostris.* Available at www.birdlife.org

British Ornithologists' Union (BOU), 2013. The British List: A Checklist of Birds of Britain. 8th edn. *Ibis* **155**, 635–675.

Chandler, R.J., 1997. Sooty Oystercatcher *Haematopus fuliginosus*: two forms or two species? *Bulletin of the British Ornithologists' Club* **117**, 158, 243.

Chandler, R.J., 2009. *Shorebirds of the Northern Hemisphere.* Christopher Helm: London.

Dowding, J.E. and Murphy, E.C., 2001. The impact of predation by introduced mammals on endemic shorebirds in New Zealand. *Biological Conservation* **99**, 47–64.

Dowding, J.E., 1994. Morphometrics and ecology of the New Zealand Dotterel (*Charadrius obscurus*), with a description of a new subspecies. *Notornis* **41**, 221–233.

Fraser, P.A., Rogers, M.J. and the Rarities Committee, 2007. Report on rare birds in Great Britain in 2005. Part 1: non-passerines. *British Birds* **100**, 16–61.

Gretton, A., Yurlov, A.K. and Boere, G.C., 2002. Where does the Slender-billed Curlew nest, and what future does it have? *British Birds* **95**, 334–344.

Hackett, S.J., Kimball, R.T., Reddy, S., Bowie, R.C.K., Braun, E.L., Braun, M.J., Chojnowski, J.L., Cox, W.A., Han, K.-L., Harshman, J., Huddleston, C.J., Marks, B.D., Miglia, K.J., Moore, W.S., Sheldon, F.H., Steadman, D.W., Witt, C.C. and Yuri, T., 2008. A phylogenomic study of birds reveals their evolutionary history. *Science* **320**, 1763–1768.

Jehl, J.R., 1975. *Pluvianellus socialis*: biology, ecology, and relationships of an enigmatic Patagonian shorebird. *Transactions of the San Diego Society of Natural History* **18**, 25–73.

Lane, B.A. and Rogers, D.J., 2000. The Australian Painted Snipe *Rostratula (benghalensis) australis*: an endangered species? *The Stilt* **36**, 26–34.

Lane, B.A., 1987. *Shorebirds in Australia.* Nelson: Melbourne.

Marchant, S. and Higgins, P.J. (eds.), 1993. *Handbook of Australian, New Zealand and Antarctic Birds, Volume 2: Raptors to Lapwings.* Oxford University Press: Melbourne.

Sangster, G., Collinson, J.M., Crochet, P.-A., Knox, A.G., Parkin, D.G., Svensson, L. and Votier, S.C., 2011. Taxonomic recommendations for British birds: seventh report. *Ibis* **153**, 883–892.

Sangster, G., Collinson, J.M., Crochet, P.-A., Knox, A.G., Parkin, D.G. and Votier, S.C., 2012. Taxonomic recommendations for British birds: eighth report. *Ibis* **154**, 874–883.

Sitters, H., Minton, C., Collins, P., Etheridge, C., Hassell and O'Connor, F., 2004. Extraordinary numbers of Oriental Pratincoles in NW Australia. *Wader Study Group Bulletin* **103**, 26–31.

Urban, E.K., Fry, C.H. and Keith, S., 1986. *The Birds of Africa, Volume 2.* Academic Press, Cambridge, MA.

2 / DRESSING FOR THE OCCASION

SHOREBIRD PLUMAGES AND MOULTS

Is that Ruff a juvenile – the first of the year? That Dunlin – is it still in breeding plumage? Why has that turnstone got such a white head? An understanding of the age and breeding status of shorebirds adds so much to one's enjoyment of them. The aim of this chapter is to help with this by providing the basic information on the different plumages worn by shorebirds, on the intervening moults during which the plumage is changed, and how the various plumages and moults cycle with the seasons.

THE SHOREBIRD PLUMAGE CYCLE

A number of different schemes have been proposed for the annual sequence of plumages and the intervening moults (see Table 1, page 90). The scheme used here is based on the *Birds of the Western Palearctic*, which avoids the terms 'summer' and 'winter' because they are potentially confusing when applied to migratory species that occur in both northern and southern hemispheres. (Note that the months given in Table 1 summarising plumage and moult periods apply specifically to the northern hemisphere.) The timing of plumages and moults of shorebirds breeding in the southern

hemisphere is very approximately the converse – by six months – of the northern hemisphere timings. Adult shorebirds that breed in the northern hemisphere are typically in breeding plumage from April to July, while those breeding in the southern hemisphere are usually in breeding plumage from September to January. A complicating factor is that species breeding close to the equator may either breed year-round or when conditions particularly suit their lifestyle, perhaps in the wet or dry seasons.

The plumage of all shorebirds is grown and then replaced by moult in a systematic manner. Chicks emerge from the egg already clad in their initial downy plumage, which dries quickly. As the chick grows, so do its feathers, with the initial down remaining at the tips of the new feathers until it gradually wears off. In the early stages of growth, the new feathers are encased in a waxy sheath, which is particularly obvious on the flight feathers, when they are referred to as being 'in-pin'. Once the first true feathers (as opposed to the initial down) are completely grown, which takes about three weeks, the bird has its first complete plumage – usually referred to as its 'juvenile' or 'juvenal' plumage. Young juvenile shorebirds, particularly the thick-knees and the small plover species, are often seen still bearing a few wisps of down on their heads or at the tips of the tail feathers.

The juvenile stage involves the only plumage where all the feathers are of the same age and so the overall impression is of a particularly neat and tidy bird. This effect is enhanced by the relatively small size of the juvenile feathers compared to those of adults and also by the neat pale fringes on the upperpart feathers of many juvenile shorebirds. Thereafter, the various plumages follow an annual sequence: juvenile, first non-breeding after about three to four months, first-breeding at 10 to 11 months, adult non-breeding plumage after about 15 months and adult breeding plumage after two years. Many of the smaller species, however, acquire adult breeding plumage within their first year.

Typically, the first non-breeding plumage is characterised by adult-type non-breeding upperpart feathers that are larger and usually plainer than the juvenile feathers they replace. First non-breeding shorebirds often retain their juvenile wing-coverts and

[Opposite] Adult Common Redshank and chick. As discussed in Chapter 5 (Shorebird Breeding and Territorial Behaviour), shorebird chicks leave their nests almost as soon as they hatch and accompany their parents, as here. This chick is in its initial downy plumage. Norfolk, UK, late June.

[Upper right] Purple Sandpiper chick. Close up, shorebird chicks are undeniably pretty, although it is usually difficult to get good views because they are adept at hiding, crouching motionless for as long as their parents continue to give alarm calls. This one is at the downy plumage stage, although its first true feathers will begin to show quite soon. Iceland, late June.

{Lower right} Young juvenile Common Ringed Plover. This individual is about three to four weeks old, at a slightly later stage than the Northern Lapwing on page 70. All its juvenile feathers are now quite well grown, although it still retains some down, particularly on the tips of its tail feathers. Both its tail and its wing feathers are still growing. Norfolk, UK, mid August.

other juvenile feathers, including flight and tail feathers, but these wear and fade, and so the pale fringes of the juvenile feathers become much less obvious. This means that careful observation is usually needed to separate first non-breeding birds from non-breeding adults of the same species. The migratory species differ as to whether they moult their juvenile body feathers before or after their first migration. Many species make their first migration in juvenile plumage and moult to first non-breeding when they reach their wintering area. Less often, they moult before migration, examples being the various North American subspecies of Dunlin (but not the European subspecies) and Double-banded Plover of New Zealand.

Most of the smaller shorebirds breed in their second year, aged ten months or so, and usually have a breeding plumage that is very similar to adult breeding. Examples are the small plovers, the stints and peeps, and other small *Calidris* species, such as Sanderling and Dunlin. Many of the larger shorebirds do not breed until they are at least two years old, for example the godwits which have non-breeding type plumage until they are ready to breed. An extreme example is the Eurasian Oystercatcher. This species does not breed until at least its fourth year – and only then does it lose its white non-breeding fore-neck collar and finally acquire its breeding plumage black throat. Even at that stage many still do not breed. Other larger species may breed aged one year, and those that do so gain full breeding plumage, as is the case for some Northern Lapwings. The Northern Lapwings that breed at one year develop black (or nearly black) faces similar to breeding adults, but at that age they still have their rather worn and faded juvenile primary feathers. Those that do not breed at one year retain the extensive white facial feathering of non-breeding birds and they do not develop the brighter breeding leg colour.

Once adult, shorebird plumages cycle between breeding and non-breeding, with intervening moults during which they acquire the next plumage. The annual major moult is at the end of the breeding season when most replace their body feathers as well as their flight feathers. In so doing, they acquire their non-breeding plumage.

[Upper left] Young juvenile Northern Lapwing. This young bird is about two to three weeks old; all its pale-fringed juvenile feathers are now growing fast, although it still retains some of its natal down at the tips of many of its new feathers. Norfolk, UK, late July.

[Lower left] Young juvenile Northern Lapwing, wing stretching; same bird as upper left The wing feathers are also well grown, although the basal shafts of the primaries are still enclosed in their waxy sheaths (i.e. they are 'in-pin'), giving the impression that there is a pale area on the outer wing. Young lapwings can fly when they are only two-thirds grown, and so it will not be long before this one is airborne. Norfolk, UK, late July.

[Upper right] Juvenile Northern Lapwing. This individual is fully grown, several weeks older than that on page 70. Compared to adults, juvenile Northern Lapwings have duller and less iridescent pale-fringed upperparts, a shorter crest and dull flesh legs, not darkish red as with adults. Norfolk, UK, mid August.

[Lower right] First non-breeding American Black Oystercatcher. This bird is acquiring plain black upperparts, but retains its neat juvenile wing-coverts. The dark eye is becoming yellow and its bill is becoming less dusky, more orange. California, USA, early November.

[Above] Juvenile Eurasian Stone-curlew. Although the cryptic juvenile plumage is very similar to that of the adult – both breeding and non-breeding – there are subtle differences, particularly the less-strongly marked face pattern of the juvenile. Norfolk, UK, late September.

[Opposite, upper] Eurasian Oystercatchers showing both breeding and non-breeding plumage. The left bird is an adult, probably a male; the right a female with a longer, more tapered bill. Since it is an early date for an adult to have a well developed non-breeding white collar, and because its bill is quite dusky at the tip, it is probably an older immature bird. Norfolk, UK, early August.

[Opposite, lower] Sanderlings – two contrasting individuals. The one in the foreground is in fresh breeding plumage, whilst the bird behind retains its non-breeding plumage. The former is probably at least two years old and will be ready to breed as soon as the conditions in the Arctic allow; the latter very grey individual is probably a second calendar-year bird, and like many at this age will probably not breed. Norfolk, UK, mid May.

At the moult to breeding plumage they mainly replace body feathers and, depending on the species, their appearance either becomes much more colourful or they remain looking much as when non-breeding. At one end of the spectrum is the Jack Snipe, which, although it moults on the annual cycle common to all shorebirds, retains a plumage that is visually identical year-round. With the other species of snipe, the initial juvenile plumage differs from that of the adult only in the wing-covert feathers; once these are replaced, after about three months, they are indistinguishable from adults.

At the other end of the range of plumage variability are Ruffs, which not only have non-breeding and breeding plumages that are visually significantly different, but there are clear differences between the sexes. To complicate matters further, the males also have an additional and relatively short-lived 'supplemental' breeding plumage when they gain the 'ruff' – and other decorative feathers – that gives the species its name. In their extraordinary supplemental breeding plumage all individual male Ruffs are different, although they can be assigned to one of three male plumage types depending on the role they adopt when displaying. The different plumages of the males and their behaviour at the lek are discussed in more detail in the context of breeding behaviour in Chapter 5.

In addition to the Ruff, it has recently been appreciated that other shorebird species, for example Great Knot, Bar-tailed Godwit and perhaps some other brightly coloured breeding species (such as Black-tailed and Hudsonian Godwits, Asian Dowitcher and Grey/Red Phalaropes), also have supplemental breeding plumages, although these plumages are less obviously different than they are in the Ruff. Consequently, these species acquire their full breeding plumage in two stages.

Some shorebird species gain 'breeding' upperpart feathers that are actually a mix of breeding and non-breeding feather types. The breeding-type feathers are grown during the pre-breeding moult, but non-breeding type feathers may be retained from the non-breeding plumage or may be grown early during the pre-breeding moult. These partial breeding plumages are often shown by the more southerly populations of species that moult earlier to enable them to breed earlier than their more northerly and later

[Right] Juvenile Black-winged Stilts. Juveniles have the pale-fringed upperparts and wing-coverts typical of many young shorebirds; they are much paler than the adults with their black upperparts and bright pink legs. Compare with adult Black-winged Stilt, page 94. Southern Spain, early September.

[Middle] Juvenile Masked Lapwing, race *novaehollandiae*. Juveniles have neatly fringed upperparts, although in this case they are dark. The wattles are smaller than in the adults, the legs are duller and the black on the head has yet to develop fully. Compare with adults, page 169. New Zealand, mid November.

[Below] Juvenile Common Snipe. All snipe species have plumages that are very similar at all ages, but juveniles (apart from Jack Snipe, which have a visually identical plumage at all ages) can be distinguished from adults by their neatly fringed wing-coverts. Once these are replaced, first-year birds are similar to adults. Norfolk, UK, early November.

[Left] Juvenile Bar-tailed Godwit. A typical juvenile plumage for a shorebird, with neat, tidy, uniformly patterned feathers. Note that the base of the bill is pink, as with all non-breeding Bar-tailed Godwits and many other closely related species. The rather long bill suggests that this may be a female. Cornwall, UK, late September.

[Middle] Juvenile Eurasian Curlew. Again, note the neat and tidy feathering. Juveniles of all the curlew species have tertials (the feathers above the folded wing tips) with deep pale notches. Cornwall, UK, mid September.

[Below] Juvenile Green Sandpiper. As this individual is in the UK, where only a few breed (in Scotland), it is likely to be a Scandinavian bird on migration to its African wintering grounds. In typical plumage for a juvenile shorebird of any species, with neat, consistently tidy, uniformly patterned feathers. Norfolk, UK, mid August.

Plumage sequence for a *Pluvialis* plover, Grey (Black-bellied) Plover. See pages 165 and 217 for other images of this species.

[Upper left] Juvenile Grey Plover with neat, strongly edgespotted upperparts. Unusually for shorebirds, all four *Pluvialis* plovers (Grey and the three golden plovers) can retain juvenile plumage well into their second calendar year, although the feathers fade and wear with time. This bird is still in fresh, highly contrasting, plumage. Florida, USA, late October.

[Upper right] First non-breeding Grey Plover. This bird has gained non-breeding-type upperpart feathers, but still has its juvenile wing-coverts and tertials. In this case the pale notches on the tertials have almost completely worn away. There is just one breeding-type black feather on its upperparts! Grey Plovers do not breed until their third calendar year, so this is a non-breeder. Norfolk, UK, mid May.

[Lower left] Adult non-breeding Grey Plover, on its European wintering grounds. Norfolk, UK, early February.

[Lower right] Adult breeding Grey Plover, no doubt on the way to its Canadian high Arctic breeding grounds. This one really is a Black-bellied Plover, as implied by its North American name! It has new black-and-white upperpart feathers, the striking black face and belly of breeding plumage, and black legs, not grey as with juveniles or non-breeding. Florida, USA, early May.

breeding congeners. Such species include Greater Sand Plover (race *columbinus*), European Golden Plover, Common Redshank, Common Greenshank, 'Western' Willet *inornata*, Asian populations of Bar-tailed Godwit *baueri*, and Temminck's Stint. The difference in plumage is particularly obvious in the southern form of European Golden Plover *P. a. apricaria*, whose face and underparts are far less dark than the more northerly and later breeding birds of the form *altifrons*. Many of the migratory species undergo the pre-breeding moult on the wintering grounds and make their return migration already largely in breeding plumage.

The shorebird species that are significant migrants have evolved moulting strategies that take their migration into account. Some breeding adults do not moult much of their breeding plumage or replace their flight feathers until they have returned to their non-breeding grounds (for example Bar-tailed Godwits of the race *taymyrensis* that fly more-or-less directly to their non-breeding area in west Africa), whilst *islandica* Black-tailed Godwits moult their body feathers while staging as they move south, although they do not moult their flight feathers until they are back in their non-breeding area. Other species may moult at least some of their flight feathers and also perhaps some body plumage while they are still breeding, for example European Golden Plovers.

GUYS AND GALS?

In most shorebird species that have a distinctive breeding plumage, the male is the more colourful of the sexes. In the smaller plovers the male often has a blacker head pattern, while with godwits, for example, the male is simply the brighter bird. The species where the female is brighter are those with polyandrous mating systems (see Chapter 5), when the less bright males have to care for the young and so need to be less conspicuous. Examples are Eurasian Dotterel, painted-snipes and phalaropes.

REVERSED PLUMAGE

Occasionally adult shorebirds are seen in breeding plumage in the non-breeding season and vice versa, having apparently 'reversed' their plumage cycle. For example, individual birds of migrant species

Plumage sequence for Double-banded Plover, a southern hemisphere small plover. Known as Double-banded Dotterel in New Zealand where they breed inland and coastally on both North and South Islands. The inland breeders – more than half the population – migrate to Australia in the Austral winter; this is one of the few breeding shorebirds in the southern hemisphere that has a significant migration. They are also relatively unusual because the juveniles moult to their first non-breeding plumage before commencing migration, not – like many shorebird species – after they arrive on their non-breeding grounds. Although they follow the usual plumage sequence for small plovers, the timing of the breeding period, and hence of its the various plumages, differs by about six months from northern hemisphere breeding species.

[Above] Juvenile Double-banded Plover showing the small, neat, pale-fringed upperpart feathers typical of shorebirds of this age. Note the paler legs compared to older birds. Coastal South Island, New Zealand, late January.

[Upper left] First non-breeding Double-banded Plover. Its juvenile pale-fringed wing-coverts have been retained, but its upperparts have new, rufous, adult-type feathers, although these will quickly become duller. The grey area on the upper breast of the juvenile has been replaced by double breast-bands and the legs have darkened. This bird is from the population that migrates to Australia. Inland South Island, New Zealand, early February.

[Lower left] Adult breeding female Double-banded Plover. Much duller than the breeding male, with restricted black on the head, upper breast-band grey not black, and less bright chestnut lower breast-band. Those individuals that migrate to Australia gain their breeding plumage before departing for New Zealand. Inland South Island, New Zealand, mid November.

[Upper right] Adult non-breeding Double-banded Plover. Uniform grey upperparts, paler below, with pale double breast-bands. Apart from a hint of darker feathering on the forehead it has the classic plain non-breeding plumage of a small plover, with no sign of the much brighter plumage of the breeding adult. Occasionally breeding females are very dull, but the date is very late in the breeding cycle and so this bird is much more likely to be in non-breeding plumage. Inland South Island, New Zealand, early February.

[Lower right] Adult breeding male Double-banded Plover. Much brighter than the breeding female. Inland South Island, New Zealand, mid November.

Plumage sequence of Dunlins. These images show the plumages of Dunlin, a small, widespread northern hemisphere shorebird that occurs widely throughout North America, Europe and Asia.

[Above] Adult Dunlin in worn breeding plumage (left) and juvenile Dunlin (right). The pale fringes of the adult's upperparts have completely worn off so it appears very dark above. The juvenile is already acquiring a few plain grey upperpart feathers of its first non-breeding plumage. Norfolk, UK, mid August.

[Left] Juvenile Dunlin, probably (from its location) of the western European race *schinzii*. Juvenile European Dunlins, unlike their North American counterparts, commence their southbound migration in juvenile plumage; the North American races moult to first non-breeding before they move south. Adult Dunlins in breeding plumage have black bellies, a plumage pattern that is mimicked by fresh-plumaged juveniles with their dense mass of black underpart spotting, as here. No other small juvenile shorebird has extensive underpart markings, and so this is a good identification feature for juvenile Dunlins. The spotting is quickly lost as they moult to first non-breeding plumage. Norfolk, England, mid August.

[Middle] First non-breeding Dunlin. This bird has lost its pale fringed scapulars and other upperpart feathers, which are replaced by larger, plain grey adult-type non-breeding feathers. The heavy spotting on the belly has also gone, but it retains its juvenile wing-coverts and tertials whose pale fringes have faded, although the basic pattern of the juvenile feathers remains and clearly contrasts with the newly acquired upperparts. This bird is of the North American race *hudsonia*, which will have gained its first non-breeding plumage before migrating south. Note the longer, slightly decurved bill of this race, recalling Curlew Sandpiper (see page 60). Florida, USA, late December.

[Below] Adult Dunlin in non-breeding plumage. The longish bill (for a European Dunlin) suggests that it is probably a female. Its upperpart feathers are similar to those of the first non-breeding bird above, with all its feathers (including the tertials and wing-coverts) plain grey and lacking the darker patterning of the feathers of the juvenile. Norfolk, UK, late March.

[Right and middle] Breeding Dunlin, race *hudsonia* from location. With this race, the breeding plumage characters are the very bright, broad chestnut mantle fringes and the relatively faint breast streaking. It is easy to see why the Dunlin in North America used to be called Red-backed Sandpiper. Again, the relatively long bill is typical of the two North American races. Dunlins breed in their second calendar year, so it is expected that they will have full breeding plumage at this age. This bird is of particular interest because it is a second-year bird, shown by the very worn, presumably juvenile wing-coverts but, unusually for this species, it has recently replaced its outer primaries. Note that the tips of the outer folded primaries are black and unworn, compared to the rather pointed tips of the (juvenile) browner inner primaries. Other small shorebirds, particularly those with long migrations, also use this strategy of partial wing-moult to replace worn juvenile outer primaries to aid their return migration. Florida, USA, mid May.

[Below] Breeding adult Dunlin, race *schinzii* from location. Dunlins are always difficult to assign to race in the field, although it is easier to do so with birds in breeding plumage. The main breeding plumage characters of this race are the broad, yellowish-red (not bright chestnut as with *hudsonia*) upperpart fringes and the moderate breast streaking, which tends to be spotted near the black belly patch. Sutherland, Scotland, UK, mid June.

[Opposite, upper right] Juvenile Burchell's Courser. The plumage sequence of all coursers is uncomplicated – juvenile, then adult. Juveniles have barred and mottled upperparts. Their head and facial patterns are dull, lacking the darker and more contrasting markings of the adults. South Africa, early November.

[Opposite, lower right] Adult Burchell's Courser. Has plain upperparts, a more strongly marked head, and a dark belly patch that is often difficult to see (as with other similarly marked coursers) due to their habit of facing slightly away from the observer when standing. South Africa, early November.

breeding in the northern hemisphere have been seen in Australasia in breeding plumage during the Austral summer. Birds that are sickly or injured often fail to attain, or only incompletely attain, breeding plumage.

CHANGES OF EYE, LEG AND BILL COLOUR

Another aspect of the plumage cycle is the change in colour of the bare parts – the eye, bill and legs. These changes occur as a consequence of increasing maturity or, with adults, as a further signal of breeding condition in addition to the acquisition of breeding plumage. All species of oystercatchers provide examples of the former – as juveniles they have rather dark eyes, dull orange bills with black towards the tip and dull coloured legs. The juveniles of the yellow-eyed oystercatchers of the Americas initially have a dark iris, but this changes to yellow as they gain first non-breeding plumage. The initially dull orange, dark-tipped bill slowly becomes brighter and more completely orange, and the dull, flesh-coloured legs gradually become pale pink, although perhaps less bright than when breeding. Similar bare-part colour changes occur in the red-eyed oystercatcher species of Europe, Asia and Australasia. The dark iris of juveniles slowly changes to red with increasing age, the dusky orange bill eventually becoming brighter orange, and the initially dull flesh legs becoming bright pink. Some adults of all species may show a darkish bill tip when not breeding.

A few shorebird species when breeding, particularly the males, have a change of colour at the bill-base that signals the acquisition of breeding condition. Examples of such colour changes include the all-dark bill developed by curlews and Bar-tailed Godwit, particularly by males, which have a pink bill base when non-breeding, and also the Black-tailed Godwit, whose non-breeding pink bill-base becomes bright orange.

Some jacanas, as well as other species, change their eye colour with age – their initially pale iris becomes quite dark in adults, which is the opposite of what happens with oystercatchers. This is the case with the Pheasant-tailed Jacana of southern Asia, and also with the two closely related American species, the Northern and Wattled Jacanas. Interestingly, although poorly recorded, the other species of

[Left] Breeding adult Common Redshank. Common Redshank is a species that can have rather variable amounts of breeding plumage on the upperparts. The nominate race *totanus*, which breeds in western Europe, rarely shows more breeding-type plumage than this individual. The heavy underpart streaks and spots are also a feature of breeding plumage. Norfolk, UK, late May.

[Middle] Breeding adult Common Greenshank. This is another species that does not always have complete breeding-type plumage. A migrant, staging on the Yellow Sea, en route northwards. South Korea, late April.

[Below] Breeding Temminck's Stint. This species shows a range of breeding-type plumages, some birds having very few dark-centred upperpart breeding feathers, whilst others have almost entirely breeding feathers. This one is about in the middle of the range of variation. Norfolk, UK, early May.

Wing-moult. This series of images helps to illustrate the various strategies used by shorebirds when undergoing wing moult. The timing of wing-moult differs between first-year birds and adults. With first-year birds the smaller species that are either sedentary or short-distance migrants will either not replace any of their juvenile wing feathers before breeding or, if migratory, may replace a few of their outer primaries before returning to their breeding areas (an example is given on page 82). The larger species, most of which do not breed until they are at least two-years old, undertake a rather leisurely wingmoult during their first summer. Thereafter, most adult shorebirds will undergo wing-moult on their non-breeding grounds.

[Above] European Golden Plovers replace some of their inner primaries on the breeding grounds; this Icelandic bird is in the early stages of this moult. The hindmost (raised) wing shows the outer five primaries, a gap and an incompletely grown dark inner primary. Also, clearly seen under the nearer wing, are the white axillaries that help to separate European from both Pacific and American Golden Plovers (which have buff-coloured axillaries). European Golden Plovers are relatively short distance migrants that will regrow the missing primaries on the breeding grounds, then suspend the moult and replace the remaining outer primaries when they reach their wintering area. Iceland, late June.

jacana apparently have similarly coloured eyes at all ages, which can be either pale (Comb-crested) or dark (African, Madagascan and Bronze-winged).

WING MOULT

For the field observer, an obvious sign of active moult is the annual dropping of flight feathers that commences at the bend of the wing – the inner primaries are lost and replaced first, followed by the outer secondaries. Initially, there is a gap in the wing-feathers at the bend of the wing, which is most obvious in flight or when the bird lifts its wings. Gradually, more flight feathers are lost, but as the feathers are regrown, the initial gap at the bend of the wing moves both towards the wing-tip with the loss of further primaries and towards the body as more secondary feathers are shed. The last primary feather to be replaced is the outer-most.

Younger shorebirds that do not breed in their second year generally start wing-moult earlier than breeding adults of the same species. Some of the smaller shorebird species that are both long-distance migrants and breed in their second calendar year have a partial wing-moult that involves just their outer two or three primaries. This strategy has evolved to replace the most worn of the juvenile wing feathers that would otherwise have to bear the brunt of the long return migration. It applies particularly to individuals that winter in the south of their non-breeding range. North American species that do this include those Least, White-rumped and Baird's Sandpipers that winter the furthest south in South America. In Europe and Asia some Sanderlings, Curlew Sandpipers and Sharp-tailed Sandpipers do the same, particularly those that winter in South Africa or Australia and breed in arctic Russia. Adults of these species have a complete moult of their flight feathers on the non-breeding grounds. Other small shorebirds, again longer distance migrants, may even have a complete wing-moult in their first non-breeding period. Examples include the strongly migratory *tundrae* race of the Common Ringed Plover, which moults its flight feathers on its African non-breeding grounds. In contrast, Common Ringed Plovers of the nominate race *C. h. hiaticula* (which do not move far from their largely European breeding grounds) do not undergo

Adult breeding Black-tailed Godwits in flight; nominate race *limosa*. Close to the breeding grounds, the lower bird is in the early stages of its wing-moult. It has dropped some inner primaries and still has its outer seven primaries. The inner-most primary has already been replaced and is quite well grown. Cambridgeshire, UK, early June.

First-summer Bar-tailed Godwit in flight. This individual is moulting its flight feathers for the first time, in its non-breeding area, well south of northern Scandinavia where it probably hatched. It is of the nominate race *L. l. lapponica*. The moult commenced a few weeks ago at the bend in the wing and is progressing outwards towards the wingtip, where the inner primaries are being regrown (a later stage of wing-moult than the bird opposite). The big gap is where the outer secondaries are being replaced. Note the contrast between the six new, darker inner primaries – two still growing, one is missing, and the remaining three faded rather brown outer primaries that are part of its original juvenile plumage, now about a year old. Compare the feathers on both wings and note that the feathering is symmetrical. It will not breed until next year and, consequently, it is in non-breeding plumage. This particular wing-moult is relatively leisurely, having started earlier in the year than with a breeding adult, and it will take another month or so to complete. Norfolk, UK, mid July.

[Above] Adult Bar-tailed Godwit on south-bound migration, still largely in breeding plumage, with an all-dark bill. This bird is of the race *taymyrensis*, which breeds on the Taymyr Peninsula in northern Russia, and will not undergo either wing- or body-moult until it reaches west Africa where it will spend the northern winter. Norfolk, UK, early August.

[Upper right] Juvenile White-backed Stilt. Aged by the neatly pale-fringed brown-black upperparts, and the not yet fully-grown bill. Lacks the white shoulders of the adult, strongly suggesting that the all-dark upperparts, shared with the North American Black-necked Stilt, is the original form. Coastal central Argentina, early December.

[Lower right] Adult White-backed Stilt. The white shoulders are unique to adult stilts of this species. The bronze-brown back, as with other stilt species, shows this is a female. Coastal central Argentina, early December.

primary moult until they are at least one-year-old and also have a body moult more-or-less directly to breeding plumage, barely acquiring its first non-breeding plumage. It therefore gains its breeding plumage significantly earlier than the migratory race *C. h. tundrae*.

A few shorebird species moult their flight feathers more-or-less simultaneously and become flightless. One of these is the African Jacana (and perhaps also the closely related Madagascan Jacana); the other jacanas all have a conventional wing-moult. A similar strategy is shown by Bristle-thighed Curlews, which also become flightless once they have returned to their Pacific island non-breeding grounds. As the Pacific islands are (or were) relatively predator-free, it is perhaps not unsurprising that these curlews have evolved a simultaneous flight-feather moult, but it is not so obvious why African Jacanas have a similar strategy.

Table 1. Terminology and timing of shorebird plumages and moults (italics are used for moult).

This book	British Birds (1985)	Humphrey and Parkes (1959)	The Birds of the Western Palearctic	Typical plumage or moult period for Northern Hemisphere breeding shorebirds	Cycle	Calendar year
Juvenile	Juvenile	Juvenile	Juvenile	June–September	1st	1st
Post-juvenile moult	Moult to first-winter or post-juvenile moult	First prebasic moult	Post-juvenile moult	August–November	1st	1st
First non-breeding	First-winter	First basic	First non-breeding	October–March	1st	1st–2nd
Moult to first-breeding	Moult to first-summer	First prealternate moult	First pre-breeding moult	March–May	1st	2nd
First-breeding	First summer	First alternate	First-breeding	April–August	1st	2nd
Moult to second non-breeding	Moult to second-winter	Second prealternate moult	First post-breeding moult	July–September	2nd	2nd
Second non-breeding	Second winter	Second basic	Second non-breeding	August–March	2nd	2nd–3rd
Moult to adult breeding	Moult to adult summer	Prealternate moult	Adult pre-breeding moult	March–May	2nd	3rd
Adult breeding	Adult summer	Definitive alternate	Adult breeding	April–August	2nd or Adult	3rd and subsequent
Moult to adult non-breeding	Moult to adult winter	Prebasic moult	Adult post-breeding	July–November	Adult	3rd and subsequent
Adult non-breeding	Adult winter	Definitive basic	Adult non-breeding	September–March	Adult	3rd and subsequent

Notes: The terminology used here largely follows that used by *The Birds of the Western Palearctic* (Cramp and Simmons 1983) and Chandler (2009). ('The 'alternate' or 'supplementary' plumage of pre-breeding Ruffs, for example, is not included. See main text for details.)

REFERENCES

Anon., 1985. Plumage, age and moult terminology. *British Birds* **78,** 419–427.

Bamford, M.J., Talbot, J., Rogers, D.I., Minton, C.D.T. and Rogers, K.G., 2005. Wader ageing series No. 1 – Red-necked Stint. *The Stilt* **48,** 28–33.

Battley, P.E., Rogers, D.I. and Hassell, C.J., 2006. Prebreeding moult, plumage and evidence for a presupplemental moult in the Great Knot *Calidris tenuirostris*. *Ibis* **148,** 27–38.

Betts, B.J., 1973. A possible hybrid Wattled Jacana ´ Northern Jacana in Costa Rica. *Auk* **90,** 687–689.

Campbell, B. and Lack, E., 1985. *A Dictionary of Birds.* T. & A.D. Poyser: Calton, UK.

Chandler, R.J., 2009. *Shorebirds of the Northern Hemisphere.* Christopher Helm: London.

Chandler, R.J. and Marchant, J.H., 2001. Waders with non-breeding plumage in the breeding season. *British Birds* **94,** 28–34.

Conklin, J.R., Battley, P.F., Potter, M.A. and Fox, J.W., 2010. Breeding latitude drives individual schedules in a trans-hemispheric migrant bird. *Nature Communications.* doi: 10.1038/ncomms1072

Cox, J.B., 1989. The measurements of Cooper's Sandpiper and the occurrence of a similar bird in Australia. *South Australian Ornithologist* **31,** 38–43.

Cox, J.B., 1990. The enigmatic Cooper's and Cox's Sandpipers. *Dutch Birding* **12** (2), 53–64.

Cramp, S. and Simmons, K.E.L. (eds.), 1983. *The Birds of the Western Palearctic,* III, *Waders to Gulls.* Oxford.

Hale, W.G., 1980. *Waders.* Collins: London.

Humphrey, P.S. and Parkes, K.C., 1959. An approach to the study of moults and plumages. *Auk* **76,** 1–31.

Jukema, J. and Piersma, T., 2000. Contour feather moult of Ruffs *Philomachus pugnax* during northwards migration, with notes on homology of nuptial plumages in scolopacid waders. *Ibis* **142,** 289–296.

Piersma, T. and Jukema, J., 1993. Red breasts as honest signals of migratory quality in a long-distance migrant, the Bar-tailed Godwit. *Condor* **95,** 163–177.

Sangster, G., 1996. Hybrid origin of Cox's Sandpiper confirmed by molecular analysis. *Dutch Birding* **18,** 255–256.

Skewes, J., Minton, C. and Rogers, K., 2004. Primary moult [also ageing] of the Ruddy Turnstone *Arenaria interpres* in Australia. *The Stilt* **45,** 20–32.

3 / FOOD, GLORIOUS FOOD!

SHOREBIRD FEEDING AND FEEDING MECHANICS

Except when breeding or actively migrating the daily preoccupation of the majority of shorebirds is either with feeding, caring for their plumage or roosting. Feeding will be a priority in the context of the daily time budget, although the time spent feeding and what is eaten will depend on the time of year (and hence the length of daylight), and whether the species feeds by sight or touch, with touch allowing the birds to feed at lower light levels and hence for a longer period of the day.

Most shorebirds have rather similar diets and they are all essentially carnivorous. As long as the food items are not too large, they will eat invertebrates of all kinds, including insects, and even small vertebrates (particularly small fish), as well as carrion. Some species, particularly those that breed in the boreal zone, will even take berries and seeds. Shorebird species that have rather different diets include the Plains-wanderer of Australia and the four species of South American seedsnipe. The latter are all mainly vegetarian, browsing on low plant growth, whilst the Plains-wanderer has a similar, but more extensive diet, taking not only leaves and seeds, but also insects and spiders. Even the biofilm that grows on coastal mudflats is exploited by a number of shorebirds, particularly the smaller *Calidris* species.

The methods used for feeding on the various food items are reflected in the obvious morphological differences between the different shorebird species, particularly in the length and shape of their bills, and to a lesser extent in the length of neck and legs, which largely control the depth of water in which the birds can feed. Those species that take food items from the ground surface or by probing to a shallow depth have short, straight bills, for example thick-knees, lapwings and plovers, jacanas, Plains-wanderer and seedsnipes, Surfbird and some of the *Calidris* sandpipers. A few specialist feeders have short but curved bills, including the Wrybill, which is unique amongst all bird species – not just the shorebirds – in having a laterally curved bill, and the coursers, which have short and slightly decurved bills.

Amongst the relatively short-billed shorebirds are some highly specialist feeders. The sheathbills and sometimes turnstones are scavengers and carrion feeders, and the specialist crab predators Crab Plover and Wilson's Plover have short but unusually heavy bills. These short-billed species are all largely visual feeders, relying on their keen eyesight to locate the majority of their food.

A few species have fairly lengthy but upturned bills, such as the avocets and Terek Sandpiper – the former primarily using their bills for sweeping through water; the latter, with head and bill held low, rapidly running down prey such as small crabs. Other shorebirds have decurved bills, including the Ibisbill, the painted-snipes, and curlews and whimbrels.

Medium-length straight bills indicate generalist shorebirds, capable of surface picking as well as probing to moderate depth in the sediment or shallow water, for example the stilts, Jack Snipe, most of the *Tringa* and *Calidris* sandpipers, and the two *Actitis* sandpipers. Long, straight or nearly straight bills indicate species that generally feed by vertical probing, although on occasion they may feed by picking. These species find most of their prey items by touch, using sensitive Herbst's corpuscles that are positioned towards the bill tip, beneath the horny keratin outer sheath of the bill. Examples are the woodcocks and snipes, dowitchers and godwits. They probe more-

Double-striped Thick-knee. All the thick-knees are
visual but largely nocturnal feeders. They have large
eyes adapted for low-light conditions, and short but
powerful bills. Venezuela, mid November.

Adult male Black-winged Stilt, feeding by picking from the water surface, the commonest feeding mode of this species. Its sex is known from its black (rather than bronze-black) upperparts; many, though not all, adult males are white headed. This bird, affectionately known as 'Sammy', first seen in late July 1993 in Northumberland, UK, arrived at the RSPB's Titchwell Marsh reserve in mid September 1993 where he became a permanent resident until his disappearance in late May 2005. Norfolk, UK, early September 2004.

[Upper] Non-breeding Wrybill showing how the unique laterally curved bill is used for feeding. It is in shallow water, sweeping the outer edge of its bill against the substrate to glean food items. The rather poorly defined black markings on forehead and breast-band are typical of non-breeding birds. This individual has probably only recently arrived in North Island from its breeding grounds in South Island. New Zealand, late January.

[Lower] Breeding adult Wrybill, feeding by picking, using its finely pointed bill. The item is a tiny ladybird. Note the blacker forehead compared to the previous image. North Island, New Zealand, mid November.

or-less vertically to access prey at depth, although species such as snipe when feeding in wet grassland will often probe forward, with their bill held at an angle of about 45 degrees. All shorebirds will, at times, probe to the full length of their bills and, when wading, will also often completely submerge their heads. The curlew species take advantage of their decurved bills to increase the chance of finding prey by twisting their bills in the substrate, as they also do when pursuing crabs within their burrows.

The small *Calidris* species include some quite specialist feeders. Red Knot (and possibly Great Knot) can detect buried shellfish by generating pressure waves in the water in the pores of the saturated substrate. They then use the Herbst's corpuscles at their bill tips to detect the rebound or echo of the pressure wave from a buried cockle, similar to how a bat uses echolocation, enabling the knot to find the cockle.

Sanderlings chase after small food items at the water's edge on sandy beaches, Western Sandpipers have 'brush-tipped' tongues that they use to graze on the thin organic surface-layer ('biofilm') of muddy sediments, and the critically endangered Spoon-billed Sandpiper hoes with its unique bill. Other specialist feeders include the phalaropes that feed almost exclusively while swimming, and which – in special, but relatively rare circumstances – use the 'spinning' technique (see later) for which they are well known.

The coursers and pratincoles are all largely insectivorous and have bills that are adapted to their particular mode of feeding. Like the lapwings and plovers, the coursers are stand–watch–run feeders and have relatively short, decurved but pointed bills, perfect for catching invertebrates on the ground. The pratincoles, in contrast, are aerial feeders that share many of the adaptations of other aerial insectivores, such as swifts and hirundines, in that they have long narrow wings and forked tails to increase manoeuvrability, and also wide gapes to aid the capture of insects.

With many shorebirds the females are usually (but not always) marginally larger than the males, and they also usually have longer bills so they can probe more deeply, thus reducing competition for food with others of their species. There is often some overlap in bill length between males and females; Bar-tailed Godwits are the only

Adult male Common Ringed Plover feeding by picking. All the lapwings and plovers are visual feeders that use the stand–watch–run technique. This bird has just paused at the end of a run to pick-up a prey item. It is of the nominate race *C. h. hiaticula*, already in breeding plumage with full bill colour; the entirely black face pattern shows that it is a male. Neither of the two migratory races of Common Ringed Plover would be in breeding plumage at this time. Norfolk, UK, late March.

[Left] Bar-tailed Godwits demonstrating the relative bill lengths of male (in front) and female (behind). In most shorebird species the females have, on average, longer bills than males, but in this species there is very little overlap in length between sexes. This adaptation has evolved to limit within-species competition for food, enabling the longer billed females to feed at greater depths. These two godwits are both largely in non-breeding plumage and so they are presumably second calendar-year birds that will not breed this year. Norfolk, UK, early May.

[Middle] Adult White-bellied Seedsnipe. All four species of seedsnipe of South America are mainly vegetarian, feeding by browsing on low vegetation. Tierra del Fuego, Argentina, early December.

[Below] Adult breeding male Black-tailed Godwit of the Asian race *melanuroides*. When not breeding Black-tailed Godwits feed in rice fields both in southern Europe and in the Far East. This one is in a newly flooded rice paddy in South Korea; the food item is perhaps the newly sprouting corm of a sedge. This is a relatively rare example of shorebirds consuming vegetable food. The strong underpart stripes are a feature of the breeding plumage of this race; the orange bill-base is also an indication of breeding condition. Western South Korea, mid May.

Adult male Shore Plover, probing for invertebrates in damp sand. This species regularly uses its longish bill (for a plover) for probing. Virtually all birds in the tiny population of this critically endangered New Zealand species are colour-ringed (see also page 197). North Island, New Zealand, mid November.

[Above] Adult Eurasian Curlew, race *N. a. orientalis*. Many shorebirds will thrust their heads well below the water's surface when wading, but in mud they probe no deeper than their bill's length, as seen here! Western South Korea, late April.

[Opposite] Adult non-breeding Common Redshank, probing face deep while keeping its eye closed! The mud on its bill and legs shows the depth of sediment in which it is probing; it has just caught a worm or something similar. The non-breeding plumage is plain brown-grey above and off-white below. Compare with the breeding adults, pages 84 and 108. Norfolk, UK, late March.

shorebird species where almost all females have longer bills than males. It has recently been discovered that their main prey items in the Dutch Wadden Sea are buried more deeply in winter, so that only the longest billed of the females remain there. The shorter billed females move to milder areas, such as The Wash in eastern England, where their prey species are less deep. This reduces competition for food within the species by forcing the shorter billed birds to move further south. The same conclusion presumably applies to the even-shorter billed males, although only females have been studied. It is quite possible that the reverse applies on the breeding grounds, with the short-billed males finding food more readily available, particularly in spring before the ground has thawed significantly.

THE FEEDING APPARATUS - BILL FLEXIBILITY

Many shorebirds have sensors – Herbst's corpuscles at their bill tips – that enable them to feed by touch. In addition, the upper mandible of their apparently rigid bill is, in fact, often remarkably flexible. This bill flexibility is most obviously seen, albeit momentarily, when shorebirds stretch their heads forward and the upper mandible flexes upward. The phenomenon is most obvious with straight-billed species, such as snipe and godwits, as seen in the accompanying images. Sinews that run from the skull along the upper mandible control the bill's flexibility, and these are probably involuntarily tightened when the bird stretches, bending the bill tip upwards.

Unlike mammals that can move only the lower jaw, all birds have the ability to move both the upper and the lower mandibles relative to the skull – 'cranial kinesis'. The main hinge is at the base of the lower mandible, but the upper mandible also has some degree of flexibility. With some bird species the upper mandible is also effectively hinged at its junction with the skull (known as prokinesis) but with most shorebirds, the upper mandible is capable of being flexed up (or down) along its length, a behaviour known as rhynchokinesis. Rhynchokinesis occurs in relatively few bird families, but it is a feature of virtually all the shorebirds, even the Wrybill with its laterally curved bill. The flexibility of the bill is probably very restricted in the oystercatchers and also with the Surfbird. In most shorebird species, particularly those with shorter

[Above] Hybrid White-headed × Black Stilt showing rhynchokinesis. The upturn of the bill seen here (and in several of the following images) is probably an unintended consequence of the controlling sinews being tensioned as the bird stretches its head forward. A major problem faced by those trying to preserve New Zealand's critically endangered Black Stilts is that they readily hybridise with the much commoner White-headed Stilts. This bird is one example, although in this case its appearance is much closer to White-headed than to Black Stilt. North Island, New Zealand, mid January.

[Opposite] The upper mandibles of the bills of most shorebirds are flexible, enabling them to be bent upwards by a surprising amount. This is 'rhynchokinesis'. The upturned mandible is of no obvious benefit – it is simply a consequence of the mechanics of the bill. What is important is that the flexibility allows the bird to bring the tips of its mandibles together, allowing it to manipulate food items, and to preen with great delicacy and precision. The lower mandible is more rigid, but is hinged where it joins the skull. These images show various shorebirds exhibiting this behaviour.

102

[Upper left] Adult breeding Sanderling, flexing its upper mandible downwards to pick up a food item – the true value of rhynchokinesis. This bird is attaining its breeding plumage, but because Sanderlings are high arctic birds that breed quite late, it will be considerably more colourful in a week or so. Norfolk, UK, mid May.

[Lower left] Marbled Godwit flexing just the tip of the bill. Florida, USA, mid September.

[Upper right] Juvenile Dunlin in the rain. In the case of the various sandpipers, snipes and woodcocks, it is largely the distal third of the bill that is flexed, as seen here. It is moulting from juvenile to first non-breeding plumage. Cornwall, UK, mid September.

[Lower right] Adult Common Snipe showing rhynchokinesis. Algarve, Portugal, late March.

Non-breeding adult Wrybill, stretching. The lapwings and plovers rarely seem to demonstrate rhynchokinesis, but when they do they flex the upper mandible fairly uniformly along most of its length. North Island, New Zealand, mid November.

Immature Great Cormorants *Phalacrocorax carbo* the right hand bird showing prokinesis for comparison with rhynchokinesis that is exhibited by shorebirds. With many bird species, as shown here – but unlike shorebirds, the upper mandible is largely rigid, but hinges at the base of the skull. Cornwall, UK, mid September.

[Left] Even though they have short bills, the lapwings and plovers also have a flexible upper mandible, which they, too, use to grasp prey items. This behaviour is even more difficult to see than with the longer billed species. This male Northern Lapwing was feeding with the stand–watch–run technique and, having seen a small prey item, it bent forward to pick it up. The enlarged detail of its bill (below) shows that the tip of the upper mandible has been flexed downwards to pick up the food item. The length of its crest, which is being blown in the breeze, shows it to be a male. Norfolk, UK, early March.

[Opposite] Juvenile Common Snipe probing vertically in soft mud to get to maximum depth. Having successfully retrieved a food item, it demonstrates the flexibility of its upper mandible as it manipulates the item prior to swallowing. This snipe is a juvenile, shown by the pale fringes around the wing-covert feathers; an adult would have paired spots at the feather tips. The juvenile wing-coverts will be replaced by adult-type feathers quite soon. Norfolk, UK, early August.

bills (including the plovers), the upper mandible bends fairly evenly along most of its length, but with the *Calidris* species and the longer billed shorebirds such as snipe, godwits and curlews, the greatest flexibility occurs in the distal third. In spite of the dramatic shape of the upward-flexed bill seen in some of the accompanying images, the main purpose of rhynchokinesis is to flex the upper mandible downwards. Together with the hinged lower mandible, this enables the bird to pick up and manipulate prey items with the bill tip, both when probing at depth in water or in sediment, and when picking from the surface. Even the short-billed seedsnipes use this ability when feeding on the vegetation that forms a major portion of their diet. The flexible bill tip is also extremely valuable when preening, but because only a minimum movement of the bill tip is required for preening it is not easily seen.

[Opposite] Adult breeding Common Redshank giving alarm calls to its young. The light was poor for photography and the exposure time was relatively long, so there is some movement blur showing that it is the lower mandible that moves when the bill is opened. Norfolk, UK, mid June.

Skulls of Eurasian Oystercatcher (a) and (c), and Eurasian Woodcock (b) and (d). The more robust bill of the oystercatcher has evolved for hammering shellfish, while the more delicate structure of the woodcock's bill enables it to exploit the flexibility of the upper mandible. The tip of an oystercatcher's bill is normally protected by about a centimetre of keratin (no longer present). The woodcock has only a minimal layer of keratin, so that in life the oystercatcher's bill would have been slightly longer than the woodcock's. The two depressions on the forehead of the oystercatcher are the locations of the salt glands, amongst the largest possessed by any shorebird. As the woodcock does not feed in a marine environment, its salt glands are small in comparison and the corresponding depressions are virtually lacking. The bill of the woodcock, particularly towards the tip, is honey-combed with small pits that are the sites of Herbst's corpuscles, providing a sense of touch that the oystercatcher does not have. The woodcock's eye sockets are set well to the side of the head, giving 360° vision.

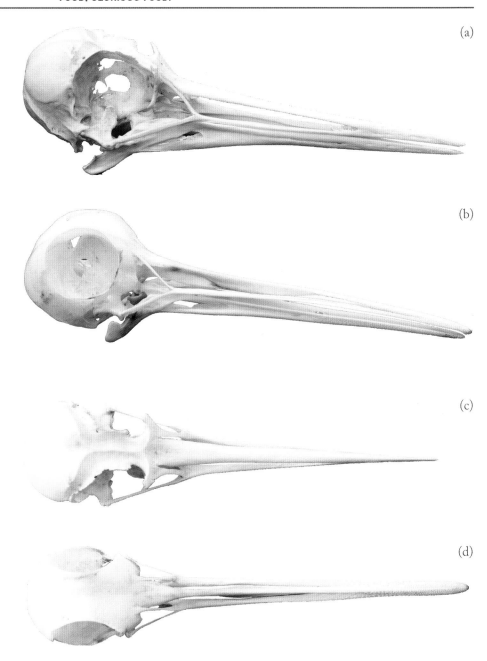

(a)

(b)

(c)

(d)

[Upper] Adult male Northern Lapwing on waterlogged ground, foot-trembling so as to disturb food items from either the vegetation or the soil close to its foot. In this case liquefaction of the substrate is unlikely to occur, prevented by the grass roots. It is vibrating its left foot; its stance is similar to the Common Ringed Plover in the next image. Norfolk, UK, late March.

[Lower] Adult male Common Ringed Plover using the foot-trembling technique to find food by liquefying the fine sand on which it is feeding, thus disturbing food items, or even cause them to float to the surface. With its weight on its left leg, it is trembling its right foot. Note that it is on the saturated area of the beach; the nearer, drier and unsaturated sand will not liquefy. The sand in front of the bird has liquefied, as shown by the slight water-filled depression in front of the plover. It is in full breeding plumage, which for the date (late February) shows that it is of the nominate race *C. h. hiaticula*, and not one of the more migratory races that do not usually acquire breeding plumage until May. Norfolk, UK, late February.

SOME FEEDING METHODS

FOOT-TREMBLING

The foot-trembling method is used by some shorebirds when feeding to disturb and thus reveal food items. This technique has been recorded being used by some lapwings and many of the plover species, but there are very few records of foot-trembling behaviour by other shorebirds. When foot-trembling, the bird stands with its weight on one leg, extends the other leg forward inclined at about 45 degrees and rapidly vibrates the forward foot, perhaps just for a second or two. The vibrating foot is held with the toes spread, either on grass or other vegetation, or on unvegetated sand or mud.

With the lapwings, foot-trembling is usually used in damp vegetation when it probably serves to disturb small insects or other food items from either the vegetation or the near-surface substrate. Plovers are usually seen foot-trembling on soft, wet, saturated sandy or muddy sediments when again the technique disturbs small invertebrates. In muddy sediments the disturbance probably results from the slight pressure waves generated in the water that fill the space between the soil particles, similar to the effect produced by the Red Knot's vibrating bill. However, with saturated, loose silt or fine sand, foot-trembling causes the substrate to liquefy briefly, and because small food items will be less dense than the liquefied sediment, they float to the surface. As liquefaction of the soil will only occur briefly, and to distances and depths that are unlikely to exceed the spread of the bird's toes, this mechanism is only likely to work at close range!

The critically endangered Shore Plover of New Zealand has, for a plover, a longish bill that it regularly uses for probing to its full length in damp sand, searching for invertebrates. It has also been observed foot-trembling to liquefy soft wet sand and, interestingly, also on moist sand (which would not be capable of liquefaction), where foot-trembling presumably serves to disturb food items in much the same way as lapwings use foot-trembling in damp vegetation.

This behaviour is very similar to the foot-trembling technique used by both Little and Snowy Egrets, which use their yellow feet in

Little Egret *Egretta garzetta* foot-trembling, using its forward (right) foot to disturb prey, watching the water closely for the appearance of food items. It has a similar stance to the shorebirds in the previous two images. Cornwall, UK, mid September.

a similar way to shorebirds to disturb food items, usually in shallow water. A somewhat similar technique is also used by gulls – foot-paddling – often in shallow water, when the gull 'marches on the spot', using both feet in succession to disturb food items which it then picks from the water.

COOPERATIVE FEEDING OR SOCIAL FORAGING

A number of bird species are known for cooperative feeding – spoonbills, herons and cormorants, amongst others. On page 114 a group of Eurasian Spoonbills is shown feeding cooperatively on tiny fish; the presence of several birds presumably panics the fish, enabling the spoonbills to catch them more easily, and perhaps even herd the fish together.

Some shorebird species use similar feeding strategies, including avocets, and two of the *Tringa* species, Spotted Redshank and Common Greenshank. Most avocets will take part in cooperative feeding when conditions allow. American Avocets do so when wading and swimming, sometimes in quite large flocks, probably hunting small fish, and Eurasian Pied Avocets have been reported feeding in a similar manner on shrimps. Red Knots nearly always feed in close association with one another; their favoured prey, small shellfish, are usually encountered in close proximity so that when one bird finds food the others quickly exploit the food source. Black-tailed Godwits often appear to be doing the same, feeding in quite closely packed groups in shallow water, probing for food in the sediment below.

TERRITORIAL BEHAVIOUR WHEN FEEDING

Territorial behaviour in shorebirds is most obvious when they are breeding – although even then the primary reason is to maintain sufficient food resources, either for the adults when nesting or for the young once they hatch. Some shorebird species, perhaps most, also show territorial behaviour out of the breeding season, again to preserve access to food. These territorial displays may last only briefly, as when one bird encroaches on the personal space of another when feeding, or they may be much longer, for example on the wintering grounds when feeding territories may be maintained

[Upper] In continental Europe, Pied Avocets feed communally in large groups, sometimes of several hundred birds. Such numbers are rarely seen in the UK, but they do feed in small groups, as here, where individual birds are taking advantage of prey items disturbed by others, increasing each bird's chances of finding food. Norfolk, UK, early March.

[Lower] American Avocets feeding co-operatively, probably attempting to catch small fish, behaviour similar to that of the spoonbills on page 114. California, USA, mid November.

[Upper left] Eurasian Spoonbills *Platalea leucorodia*, another bird species that sometimes feeds co-operatively, feeding on small fish. There were about eight to ten spoonbills in this group, all feeding quite successfully, regularly tossing their heads up (as the right-hand bird is doing) whenever they caught a fish. As a group they worked systematically back and forth through the water, apparently driving the fish before them. Norfolk, UK, early August.

[Lower left] Non-breeding Black-tailed Godwits (race *islandica*) feeding in fresh water, in typical manner, probing vertically below the water surface. They often feed in quite close groups, apparently attracted to where their congeners are feeding. Red Knots behave similarly. Norfolk, UK, late September.

[Upper right] Black-tailed Godwits probe continuously for several seconds, then when they encounter a food item the bill is lifted from the water so that they can swallow – or perhaps just take a breath! The nearer bird is a male, still in breeding plumage with the orange bill-base of breeding birds, that has probably only recently returned from its breeding grounds in Iceland. The bird behind is a non-breeding, probably second-summer bird, with a pink bill-base, having spent the northern summer where it was photographed. The chance of two adjacent godwits lifting their bills simultaneously is quite low! Norfolk, UK, late August.

[Lower right] Non-breeding Red Knots feeding as a group. As with Black-tailed Godwits, Red Knots are attracted to others of the same species that are already successfully feeding. When probing, Red Knots use the Herbst's corpuscles at their bill tips to detect waves of water pressure reflected from buried shellfish. This sensing technique will only work when the water surface is at or above that of the sediment, as here. Florida, USA, late December.

[Above] Common Ringed Plovers in territorial dispute when feeding. A short-lived event, over as soon as the second bird moved away. It is interesting that they have similar postures to those used by breeding adults when distracting potential predators (see page 195). Both birds are juveniles, probably of one of the migratory races, moving south for the winter. Cornwall, UK, mid September.

[Oppsoite, right] Semipalmated Plovers in territorial dispute when feeding. This is very similar to displays given by Common Ringed Plovers, as above. Adult left, juvenile right. Florida, USA, late August.

[Opposite, middle] Adult 'Hudsonian' Whimbrel (the North American race) giving its bubbling call, directed at a juvenile of the same species that is just out of picture. All species of curlew can be quite territorial on their feeding grounds, reacting with a musical, bubbling call to other con-specifics that encroach on what they regard as 'their patch'. Northern Chile, mid November.

[Opposite, below] Adult Eurasian Curlew giving the bubbling territorial call, flying to confront an intruder. Norfolk, UK, early March.

for weeks or even months. Grey Plovers, Common Redshanks and particularly curlews are examples of species that may hold territory for extended periods, even though nearby birds of the same species may feed quite happily together.

NOCTURNAL FORAGING

Some shorebirds regularly feed at night, perhaps the best known of these being the thick-knees with their huge eyes, but also Crab Plover, Inland Dotterel of Australia, the various woodcock and snipe species, and the *Rhinoptilus* coursers. Coastal species are affected by tidal conditions, particularly during the winter months when the day length is short, and so they feed at night to maximise the time they can spend on exposed intertidal areas. Such species include oystercatchers, Sanderlings and Dunlins, but lapwings and the *Pluvialis* plovers have optical adaptations that allow them to feed even when it is quite dark. Earlier ideas that they only feed near the full moon – although this may be helpful – are not correct, and the excellent night vision of lapwings and plovers enables them to take advantage of the larger prey, particularly earthworms, which are more available and more easily caught at night. Thick-knees have been shown to have even more sensitive retinas than lapwings, as might perhaps be expected for a specialist nocturnal feeder.

EATING CRABS

Many shorebirds will eat crabs (not just the specialist crab predators) if they encounter them. The crabs taken depend partly on their size, on the size of the shorebird, and on the bird's feeding situation. A crab may be caught in a more-or-less chance encounter while looking for food by deliberate probing for crabs under stones, by probing down a burrow (particularly with curlews and whimbrels), and even by probing under water. Once caught, the crabs are often swallowed whole, but often the claws and legs are removed if the entire crab is too large to swallow. In the latter case, the crab is picked up by a leg or claw, shaken until the leg or claw is detached, then picked up again, and the process repeated until the bird is able to swallow the body with any remaining legs or claws. At early stages of the de-legging process it is more often a claw rather than a leg that is

[Opposite, upper left] Adult male American Oystercatcher with a crab. The crab's legs have been removed, and the bird is moving the body to a firm substrate where it can hammer at the soft underbelly. Race *durnfordi*. Northern Argentina, late November.

[Opposite, lower left] Adult male American Oystercatcher. The same bird as the previous image, eating the crab. This shows that even the relatively rigid bills of oystercatchers have some flexibility! Northern Argentina, late November.

[Upper right] Adult Wilson's Plover, with a small crab. Wilson's Plovers are crab specialists and, as a result, have evolved a relatively heavy bill. Florida, USA, mid June.

[Lower right] Juvenile Whimbrel, race *phaeopus*. As well as picking and probing, Whimbrels will reach under stones, twisting their decurved bills, searching for small crabs and similar food items. This juvenile was apparently unsuccessful in its search, despite it probing under several stones. Cornwall, UK, mid September.

[Opposite] Adult Whimbrel eating a crab. It was almost high tide, and this Whimbrel was working a seaweed covered area, paying particular attention to angular stones that were close to the highest extent of the bladder wrack. It probed under the stones, and captured several small crabs; they had shells perhaps two to three centimetres across, too large for it to swallow with legs attached. It proceeded to remove the legs and claws by holding each in turn and shaking the crab until the appendage came off, repeating the process until most, if not all, the legs and claws had been removed. It then swallowed the carapace and any remaining legs whole. With several of the crabs it subsequently picked up at least some of the previously discarded claws and legs and swallowed these too. Cornwall, UK, mid September.

[Right] When shaking claws and legs from the body of a crab it is often the claws that are grasped first, most probably because crabs instinctively raise them in defence and so they are most easily grasped. Swallowing a crab usually results in the bird closing its eye! Cornwall, UK, mid September.

[Opposite] Adult Eurasian Curlew eating a crab. This curlew fed nearby for well over an hour on a falling tide. Initially it was probing the estuarine mud for ragworms or similar, of which it caught a number. Then it moved to the stream that flowed into the estuary. The current was quite fast, but with a depth that allowed the curlew to wade. Note the strong flow of water from left to right, past the bird's legs. A few minutes after entering the water it caught a small crab which it swallowed whole, and then, over the next ten minutes or so, it caught two or three others, all of similar size. Then it moved back to the estuary mud to continue searching for ragworms. It appeared that it had deliberately moved to the stream once it was of a depth where it could wade comfortably and had chosen crabs of a size that it could swallow whole, because by removing the legs it would have lost the crabs to the fast flowing water. Presumably it had disturbed all the crabs it was likely to find in the restricted area in which it was feeding, and so moved back to feed on the mud. Cornwall, UK, mid September.

[Right] Adult Eurasian Curlew eating a crab. It removed the crab's claws and legs in the same manner as the Whimbrel on pages 120 and 121, and made good use of its flexible upper mandible to manipulate its prey. Cornwall, UK, mid September.

grasped. It is not clear if this is to get rid of the more threatening and bulky claws as soon as possible, or if it is simply that the crab raises its claws to defend itself, and these are most easily grabbed by the bird. Oystercatchers differ in the way they consume larger crabs; having removed the legs as described, they chisel through the crab carapace to get at the flesh.

INSECTS AS FOOD

Most, if not all, shorebird species will take insects if the opportunity arises. Usually this is on the breeding grounds where, for arctic breeding species, insects can be numerous and where they probably form a staple item of diet for the chicks that have to feed for themselves as soon as they hatch. One or two species are effectively insect specialists – a particular example is the Puna Plover of South America, which breeds at saline oases or wetlands in the Atacama Desert, high in the Andes. There, brine flies *Ephydra* spp. are extremely numerous and provide a ready food supply, although it is unlikely that the flies are their sole food source. The Puna Plovers share their saline wetland habitat with Andean Avocets, which also probably take the brine flies and their larvae, but also feed, in the usual avocet bill-sweeping manner, on brine shrimps.

[Above] Salar de Atacama. A very large saline wetland just west of the main Andean chain, at an altitude of about 2,300 m. It is home to Andean Avocets and Puna Plovers, as well as small numbers of non-breeding visitors from North America such as Baird's Sandpipers. The peaks behind are volcanoes, part of the Andes. Northern Chile, mid November.

[Opposite] Adult breeding male Puna Plover catching brine flies. Brine flies are numerous on the saline wetlands of Chile's Atacama Desert, and provide a good food source for shorebirds, including the local breeders such as Puna Plovers and Andean Avocets. As with most small plovers, male Puna Plovers have blacker, more contrasting face patterns. Salar de Atacama, Northern Chile, mid November.

[Opposite] Adult Wattled Jacana, a 'picker', taking a small green grasshopper. Venezuela, mid November.

[Right] Adult breeding male Black-tailed Godwit, race *islandica*, catching flies. Iceland, late June.

[Middle] Juvenile Common Sandpiper flycatching. Norfolk, UK, late August.

[Below] Collared Pratincole in flight. Convergent evolution has resulted in pratincoles strongly resembling and feeding in a similar manner to the (completely unrelated) but also insectivorous hirundines, such as the Barn Swallow *Hirundo rustica* and House Martin *Delichon urbicum*. Cyprus, late April.

[Left] Adult Madagascan Pratincole. As with all the swallows, pratincoles have wide mouths to aid catching insects. The short tail of this species results in the wings extending well beyond the tail tip. This is one of the few shorebirds that migrate entirely within the southern hemisphere, breeding in Madagascar then moving across the Indian Ocean to East Africa. Madagascar, early December.

[Middle] Madagascan Pratincole in flight. The relatively short tail of this species is only slightly forked. Madagascar, early December.

[Below] House Martin *Delichon urbicum*, an image to emphasise their convergent similarity to pratincoles. Norfolk, UK, late May.

SOME SPECIALIST FEEDERS

OYSTERCATCHERS

Although they have relatively long straight bills and often probe, oystercatchers as their name suggests, can be quite specialist in their feeding. Younger birds, as well as those that breed in wet meadows away from the coast, regularly feed by probing but others, mainly older birds, use their bills as chisels, particularly when feeding on shellfish. Individual oystercatchers differ in whether they are probers or chisellers, and as a consequence their bill shapes reflect their feeding mode – pointed in probers but much more square-tipped in chisellers. It takes some time to learn the knack of chiselling, and so chisellers tend to be older birds. Moreover, individuals that winter on the coast may be chisellers, but revert to being probers in spring and summer if they breed inland and feed in damp meadows. The shape of the bill tip is a consequence of the continuous growth, at a rate of about 3 mm per week, of the keratin sheath that covers the bony inner core of the bill. The keratin tip of the bill, which is about 10 mm long, is worn away in the feeding process, resulting in a shape that reflects the individual's current feeding mode. In particular, the various species of black oystercatcher, which are rocky coast specialists and thus regularly use their bills on hard surfaces, often have noticeably blunt or square-tipped bills.

Oystercatchers use two techniques when preying on shellfish, particularly mussels. If mussels are found partly open in shallow water the bird will open the shell *in situ* by stabbing, severing the adductor muscles. Alternatively, it will remove mussels from the substrate, take them to a firm stratum where it will open the shells at the hinge by hammering.

AVOCETS

The upturned bills of avocets, although finely pointed at the tip, are broader at the base and have a fine lamellar structure to filter the minute food items that they encounter as they feed. They usually feed while wading, scything the bill back and forth just below the water surface. They have webbed feet and swim readily, sometimes sweeping the bill as they do when wading, but they will also probe

Adult American Oystercatcher eating a bivalve shellfish. This is a female as shown by the dark flecking that makes the iris appear oval and by its relatively long and slender bill. The bivalve was probably found gaping in shallow water and is being consumed *in situ*, one of two different techniques used by oystercatchers to eat bivalve molluscs. Florida, USA, mid December.

[Upper left] Adult male American Black Oystercatcher, a shorebird of the rocky coast of western North America. This bird can be identified as a male from its relatively short, deep bill and circular, rather than oval, iris. The chisel-tipped bill has been worn into that shape as a result of feeding on shellfish in its rocky habitat. California, USA, early November.

[Upper right] First-breeding (second calendar-year) Eurasian Oystercatcher feeding on grassland. It has the broad white collar, greyish legs and dark eye of an immature. The dusky-tipped, pointed bill is typical of this age and shows that it is a 'prober'. Its prey item is a leatherjacket, the pupa of a cranefly, probably *Tipula paludosa*. Sutherland, UK, early June.

[Lower left] Adult Pied Avocet, feeding by probing. Despite its specialised, upturned bill, here it is probing for ragworms or similar, as do many of the longer billed shorebirds. Norfolk, UK, mid May.

[Lower right] Adult Pied Avocet feeding by bill sweeping. Avocets' bills have a fine lamella structure that filters tiny food items as it sweeps its bill through the water. This one has something slightly bigger – a small fish. Lincolnshire, UK, mid May.

down to the sediment surface, up-ending like dabbling ducks, their bills propelled downward by strong thrusts by their webbed feet. Although bill sweeping while wading is their primary feeding mode – for which their upturned bills have evolved – avocets also feed by picking and probing on or in muddy sediments, even bill-sweeping in liquid mud. They will also take any small fish or similar items they may encounter.

LAPWINGS AND PLOVERS

The lapwings and plovers, all of which are short-billed, are typical shorebird pickers, using the stand–watch–run technique, in which they pause to look for food on or close to the ground surface, waiting for some telltale movement, and then quickly run and tilt forward to pick up the food item. The majority of their food is taken in this manner.

The Wrybill, a small plover of New Zealand, has a sideways curved bill (turned through about 12 degrees, always to the right) that is adapted for probing under pebbles. It feeds in shallow water with sideways flicks of its head, using the outer edge of its curved bill to glean food items from submerged surfaces just below the water level. It also regularly uses its fine-tipped bill – very delicately – for picking.

BRUSH-TIPPED TONGUES – WESTERN AND OTHER SMALL SANDPIPERS

A number of shorebirds, of which the Western Sandpiper of North America is the most studied, have evolved brush-tipped tongues that enable them to feed on the biofilm on the surface of coastal mudflats. The biofilm can be up to 2 mm thick, and is a reasonably coherent organic mat that, if disturbed, becomes liquid. This is the result of the forming and breaking of the polymer chains that lightly reinforce the biofilm and thus maintain its stability, even during rain or when covered by the tide. This property of the biofilm is exploited by Western Sandpipers who use a rapid stitching movement of their bill tips to fluidise the biofilm, which is then consumed using the brush-tipped tongue. Species known to have brush-tipped tongues include Kentish, Lesser Sand and Grey Plovers, several of the *Calidris* sandpipers and close relatives, and several *Tringa* and their

[Opposite] Adult female Eurasian Oystercatcher moving a mussel so that it can hammer the shell open. This is the other of the two techniques used by oystercatchers when feeding on bivalves. This bird is of particular interest because it lacks the white collar of non-breeding plumage that most Eurasian Oystercatchers have in mid December. The number (FA11122) on its ring was read from several different photographs. It was already an adult when ringed, and thus at least 22 years old when photographed. At this time of the year the vast majority of Eurasian Oystercatchers have the non-breeding white fore-neck collar, although it is absent in about 5% of birds. Presumably, as with this bird, they are some of the oldest in the population. Norfolk, UK, mid December.

[Right] (top) Eurasian Curlews, like all other curlews, make good use of their decurved bills when feeding, simultaneously twisting and probing, and so searching a larger volume of the substrate with a single probe than is possible with the straight bill of a snipe or godwit. (middle) Having encountered a ragworm, it pulled firmly but gently to extract the complete worm, and then (bottom) turned to the nearest water to wash it before swallowing. An adult of the European race *aquata*. Norfolk, UK, early March.

[Opposite, upper left] Adult non-breeding Common Greenshank, fishing. Greenshanks are a favourite shorebird for many. They always appear so elegant and are exciting to watch, particularly if they are chasing small fish (Three-spined Stickleback *Gasterosteus aculeatus* in this case) through the shallows. It caught several as I watched. Common Greenshanks breed no closer to this location than Scotland, and do not breed until their third calendar-year. As this one is already in non-breeding plumage it is probably a second-year bird that migrated at least part way back towards its breeding grounds, and is now returning south to winter in Africa. Norfolk, UK, late August.

[Opposite, upper right] Sadly, the Common Greenshank's feeding site in the previous image was overwhelmed by a large storm in the North Sea in December 2013. The coastal shingle bank was overtopped and extensive portions of it were washed inland. Many little pools behind the bank along this part of the coast were filled in, and although a few remain, they no longer appear to be as attractive to shorebirds as before. Norfolk, UK.

[Opposite, lower left] Willet – another shorebird with a fish. This is the largest *Tringa* species. The worn wing-coverts and brownish tertials are retained juvenile feathers, and so this bird is in first-breeding plumage. Willets probably do not breed until they are in their fourth calendar-year. Florida, USA, early April.

[Opposite, lower right] Adult non-breeding Greater Yellowlegs. The apparent water droplet at the bill tip is a water snail egg, a food item often taken by shorebirds. Florida, USA, late December.

[Upper right] Close-up of water snail eggs; these are a fresh water species. Scale in mm. Northamptonshire, UK, mid April.

[Lower right] Juvenile Ruddy Turnstone excavating in the beach, searching for small invertebrates such as sand hoppers. Note the spray of sand it is throwing up with the toss of its head. Cornwall, UK, mid September.

[Opposite] Adult breeding male Ruddy Turnstone, levering with its bill to move a stone, looking for food. It was probably breeding in Greenland or northern Canada little more than a week earlier! Norfolk, UK, early August.

[Above] Adult non-breeding Black Turnstone. A shorebird restricted to rocky shores of the North American Pacific coast. The soles of their feet and toes, as with Ruddy Turnstone, are cushioned, an adaptation to their rocky habitat that is similar to (but less so than) the feet of Surfbird (see page 154). California, USA, mid November.

close relatives. Although the larger species may use their specially adapted tongues to consume biofilm, it is probably only a major food item for the smaller species such as the stints and peeps.

SPOON-BILLED SANDPIPER

Perhaps the most curious bill of all shorebirds is that of the Spoon-billed Sandpiper, which it uses by 'hoeing' as it moves forward, taking in small food items. It seems to prefer to feed in shallow water at the edge of small pools, shovelling briefly in the sediment just below the water surface as if to test for food items, and then moving on to test elsewhere, again just below the water surface. There is a slight point at the centre of the blade of the hoe that appears to allow it to direct the discharge of water from its bill as it feeds.

PHALAROPES

Phalaropes of all three species usually feed while swimming; they turn rapidly and randomly, left and right, pecking small food items from the water surface. As many as 180 pecks per minute have been reported for a Red-necked Phalarope. Wilson's Phalaropes sometimes walk and pick from the water's edge, but even they more usually swim. All three species are well known for 'spinning' while feeding, although in fact they do so rather rarely and only under certain very specific conditions. The true spinning behaviour (rather than random multi-directional surface picking) involves the phalarope spinning rapidly and continuously, either clockwise or counter-clockwise. Rates of rotation in the range 38–58 revolutions per minute and up to 308 consecutive rotations have been recorded!

Anyone who has watched a phalarope feed by random picking immediately realises that even their normal feeding method must consume a good deal of energy. Spinning, however, is reported to use four times more energy than their usual surface picking. The spinning phalarope produces a vortex of water that pulls food items from below the bird, and it is therefore no surprise that it works best in shallow water, usually at depths well under a metre where food items are to be found. Given the energy expenditure, spinning is only likely to occur if sufficient food is not available with the bird's usual feeding style, and it is not surprising that phalaropes spin infrequently.

Western Sandpipers feeding on a mud flat, utilising their brush-tipped tongues to mop up the surface biofilm liquefied by the rapid stitching motion of their bills and tongues. Note that all the sandpipers are feeding by holding their bill-tips just below the surface; none has probed more deeply or raised its bill tip above the level of the biofilm. All are adults in non-breeding plumage. Florida, USA, mid November.

[Upper and middle right] Spoon-billed Sandpiper. First it shovelled briefly in the sediment just below the water surface, searching for food items, and then moved on to repeat the action. The slight point at the centre of the lower edge of its bill appears to enable it to direct the discharge of water as it feeds. Adult, breeding plumage, on northward migration. Western South Korea, late May.

[Lower right] Low tide feeding habitat used by Spoon-billed Sandpiper at the margins of the Yellow Sea. The bird in the two previous images fed along the edge of these small pools. South Korea, late May.

Another feeding technique used by phalaropes, and perhaps other shorebird species, is to exploit the surface tension of water to help them ingest small food items. A small food item picked from the water surface inevitably comes with a slightly larger globule of water, and so when the bird opens its bill the water containing the food item is pulled up the bill to the mouth by surface tension. One might expect this technique to work best for the relatively narrow-billed Red-necked and Wilson's Phalaropes, but it also seems to work just as well for the broader-billed Grey Phalarope, as seen in the accompanying images.

TURNSTONES

Turnstones of both species – Ruddy that occurs coastally almost worldwide and Black Turnstone of the rocky North American Pacific coast – have short, robust, pointed bills. Both are simultaneously generalist and specialist feeders. As generalists, they pick from the ground surface and probe to shallow depths but, as their name suggests, their speciality is to actively overturn stones, seaweed and anything else they can move that might conceal food items. They will even occasionally dig in the beach using their robust bills in search of prey items such as sandhoppers, and in the process they can excavate surprisingly large holes.

[Above] First non-breeding Grey Phalarope, picking food items from the water surface, showing its use of the surface tension of the water droplet that contains the food item. As it opens its bill, the water droplet moves upwards to its mouth, to be swallowed. Aged by the plain, pale grey adult-type upper-part feathers and the retained juvenile white-fringed near-black tertials (just above the tail), which contrast with the darker, rather worn wing-covert feathers. Cambridgeshire, UK, early October.

[Opposite] Wilson's Phalarope. As with the above photograph, the bird is using the surface tension feeding technique. It can be aged as first non-breeding by the plain, pale, newly grown grey adult-type upper-part feathers that contrast with the browner, rather worn juvenile wing-covert feathers. Northern Chile, mid November.

DRINKING

Curiously, shorebirds are rarely seen drinking, but when they drink they do so in the same manner as most other bird species – by dipping the bill to scoop up water and then raising the head to swallow. Perhaps it is not surprising that they are rarely seen drinking; much of their prey is quite moist and many species feed in such a way that ingesting water must be almost unavoidable. One situation in which shorebirds are seen drinking is when they have just completed a long migration flight – when dehydration is to be expected!

[Above] Black-tailed Godwit drinking. Shorebirds drink in the same manner as most other birds, bending forward to scoop up water, then raising the head and neck so that gravity assists the swallowing process. Adult breeding male, race *islandica*. Iceland late June.

[Opposite] Adult Eurasian Curlew drinking. It is low tide and the stream in which it is feeding is probably largely, if not completely, fresh water. Cornwall, UK, mid September.

DISCARDING THE TRASH – PELLETS

Some shorebirds, particularly curlews and godwits, may wash dirty food items such as ragworms that they have extracted from the mud. They generally do this only if they are quite close to puddles of surface water. Then they will dabble the worm in water before swallowing; it is presumably not energy efficient to walk very far to get to water for this purpose. As well as dirt from their food, shorebirds also take in indigestible matter such as crab and mollusc shells. Such material may later be brought up as a pellet ejected through the mouth, usually after coughing or retching movements that may last for several minutes. When this happens the bird generally stands still and may appear to be in some discomfort.

[Above] Adult Sanderling, bringing up a pellet of indigestible material. After standing in the same place for several minutes, coughing periodically, it opened its bill wide, allowing the pellet to drop onto the sand in front of it. It is moulting from breeding to non-breeding plumage. Florida, USA, early September.

REFERENCES

Armitage, I., 2008. Foot-trembling and beak probing by the shore plover (*Thinornis novaeseelandiae*) on sandy beaches. *Notornis* **55,** 38–39.

Burton, P.J.K., 1972. Some anatomical notes on the Wrybill. *Notornis* **19,** 26–32.

Cestari, C., 2009. Foot-trembling behavior in Semipalmated Plover *Charadrius semipalmatus* reveals prey on surface of Brazilian beaches. *Biota Neotropica* **9,** 299–301.

Chandler, R.J., 2002. Rhynchokinesis in waders. *British Birds* **95,** 395–397.

Chandler, R.J., Everett, M., Palmer, P. and Porter, R., 2015. The spinning behaviour of phalaropes. *British Birds* **108,** 104–108.

Cunningham, S.J, Corfield, J.R, Iwaniuk, A.N, Castro, I., Alley, M.R, Birkhead, T.R. and Parsons, S., 2013. The anatomy of the bill tip of Kiwi and associated somatosensory regions of the brain: comparisons with shorebirds. *PLoS ONE* **8** (11): e80036. doi: 10.1371/journal.pone.0080036

del Hoyo, J., Elliott, A. and Sargatel, J. (eds.), 1996. *Handbook of the Birds of the World. Volume 3: Hoatzin to Auks.* Lynx Editions: Barcelona.

Duijns, S., van Gils, J.A., Smart, J. and Piersma, T., 2015. Phenotype-limited distributions: short-billed birds move away during times that prey bury deeply. *Royal Society Open Science* **2,** 150073. http://dx.doi.org/10.1098/rsos.150073

Elner, R.W., Beninger, P.G., Jackson, D.L. and Potter, T.M., 2005. Evidence of a new feeding mode in western sandpiper (*Calidris mauri*) and dunlin (*Calidris alpina*) based on bill and tongue morphology and ultrastructure. *Marine Biology* **146,** 1223–1234.

Fraser, P.A., Rogers, M.J. and the Rarities Committee, 2007. Report on rare birds in Great Britain in 2005. Part 1: non-passerines. *British Birds* **100,** 16–61.

Gillings S. and Sutherland W.J., 2007. Comparative diurnal and nocturnal diet and foraging in Eurasian Golden Plovers *Pluvialis apricaria* and Northern Lapwings *Vanellus vanellus* wintering on arable farmland. *Ardea* **95,** 243–257.

Heppleston, P.B., 1971. Feeding techniques of the Oystercatcher. *Bird Study* **18,** 15–20.

Kuwae, T., Miyoshi, E., Hosokawa, S., Ichimi, K., Hosoya, J., Amano, T., Moriya, T., Kondoh, M., Ydenberg, R.C. and Elner, R.W., 2010. Variable and complex food web structures revealed by exploring missing trophic links between birds and biofilm. *Ecology Letters.* doi: 10.1111/j.1461-0248.2012.01744.x

Marín, G., Rojas, L.M., Ramírez, Y., McNeil, R. and Figueroa, L., 2012. Retinal morphology and electroretinography in two visually foraging charadriiformes birds with different feeding activity rhythms: the Double-striped Thick-knee (*Burhinus bistriatus* Wagler, 1829) and the Southern Lapwing (*Vanellus chilensis* L., 1758). *The Biologist (Lima)* **10,** 6–23.

Mathot, K.J., Lund, D.R. and Elner, R.W., 2010. Sediment in stomach contents of Western Sandpipers and Dunlin provide evidence of biofilm feeding. *Waterbirds* **33,** 300–306.

McNeil, R. and Rodriguez S., J.R., 1996. Nocturnal foraging in shorebirds. *International Wader Studies* **8,** 114–121.

Simmons, K.E.L., 1961a. Foot-movements in plovers and other birds. *British Birds* **54,** 34–39.

Simmons, K.E.L., 1961b. Further observations on foot-movements in plovers and other birds. *British Birds* **54,** 418–422.

van de Kam, J., Ens, B., Piersma, T. and Zwarts, L., 2004. *Shorebirds. An Illustrated Behavioural Ecology.* KNNV Publishers: Utrecht, The Netherlands.

4 / 'WHEN AH ITCHEZ, AH SCRATCHEZ!'
PLUMAGE MAINTENANCE AND SHOREBIRD PHYSIOLOGY

COMFORT BEHAVIOUR

Regular plumage maintenance – often referred to as 'comfort behaviour' – is something all species of birds need to do and it occupies a significant portion of their daily time budget. The various items of plumage maintenance include bathing, preening, wing-stretching, scratching and perhaps even simply resting or 'loafing'.

BATHING

Bathing is often a preliminary to preening – it helps to remove dust and dirt from the plumage, and for preference usually takes place in fresh water. Shorebirds usually choose to bathe in relatively shallow water where, by simply flexing their legs, they can largely or completely immerse themselves while simultaneously spreading and flapping their wings, splashing vigorously. After dunking themselves a few times they either remain standing in the water to preen, or they may move a short distance from the water's edge where they often choose to preen while standing close to a clump of grass or similar vegetation.

PREENING

Preening serves three main purposes: to restore feather structure, to waterproof the plumage and to control feather lice and other parasites. The shorebird systematically uses the tip of its bill to restore its feather structure by reconnecting the barbs on the individual feather filaments, opening its bill slightly and then delicately flexing the upper mandible to bring its bill tips together. If they preen standing in water they will often dip the tip of their bill in the water to wet their plumage further.

Mutual preening, or allopreening, where two individuals of the same species simultaneously preen one-another, usually the head and neck where it is difficult for a single individual to reach, has apparently not been recorded for shorebirds, although it might seem appropriate for the longer billed species such as snipe and curlews to do so! This is perhaps not surprising because allopreening is most frequent in colonies of densely nesting communal species, a breeding strategy shown by very few shorebirds.

Another objective of preening is to waterproof the plumage, which is done with the use of the preen gland, situated on the lower rump just above the tail. The preen gland releases a waxy oil that all birds work into their plumage to help waterproof the feathers. It probably also improves the flexibility of feathers and reduces wear. The gland is gently manipulated by the bill to extrude preen oil, which is either spread directly onto the feathers with the bill tip or indirectly by vigorously rubbing the back of the head against the gland and then transferring the preen oil from the head to other parts of the plumage.

For most of the year the chemical composition of the preen oil is mainly of relatively volatile compounds, but for a short period in the breeding season, ending when hatching occurs, the components change to be more viscous and less volatile. These chemical changes apply to both temperate and arctic breeding shorebirds. The most likely explanation for this phenomenon is that the less volatile compounds are likely to reduce the smell of incubating birds, and so reduce the chances of being detected by predators, such as Red Fox *Vulpes vulpes*. Support for this is provided by the observation that with two shorebird species where the male does not incubate,

Shorebirds bathing. These images show typical shorebird bathing behaviour. They usually use fresh water of sufficient depth to more-or-less completely immerse themselves if they flex their legs, but shallow enough to stand above water level when they straighten them again.

[Upper Left] Common Snipe bathing.
Adult. Norfolk, UK, early November.

[Lower left] Eurasian Curlew bathing. The relatively short bill suggests a male; it is probably only males that acquire an all-dark bill when breeding, as has this bird. Females and non-breeders have a pink bill-base. Poland, late April.

[Upper right] Marbled Godwit bathing.
Adult. Florida, USA, early October.

[Lower right] Juvenile Bar-tailed Godwit. After bathing it stretched and shook both its wings before moving out of the water to preen. Cornwall, UK, mid September.

This series of images shows shorebirds preening, first applying preen oil, then delicately using their bill tips to restore the feather structure, some while standing in water, others out of the water, but often not far from it!

[Left] American Oystercatcher preening. Bathing is often followed by a preening session. One of the reasons for preening is to renew waterproofing of the plumage. Shorebirds do this by gently squeezing their preen gland situated just above the tail to extrude preen oil, which is then worked into the feathers. This individual is an adult, probably a male from the near circular iris; note the yellow eye and dull, pale pink legs common to all adult oystercatchers of the Americas. Florida, USA, early May.

[Middle] Adult Eurasian Oystercatcher preening, working the preen oil that it has just extruded onto the back of its head, which it will then transfer to other parts of its plumage. Caithness, UK, mid June.

[Below] Adult Eurasian Oystercatcher preening, transferring preen oil from the back of it head to where it was needed. Caithness, UK, mid June.

[Opposite] Ruddy Turnstones preening. The right-hand bird is exposing its preen gland at the base of the tail. There is not enough plumage of the right-hand bird visible to enable it to be aged, but the left-hand bird is in its second calendar-year, acquiring the reddish-edged scapulars of its first-breeding plumage, but retaining worn, neatly pale-fringed juvenile wing-coverts. Norfolk, UK, early March.

[Upper left] Northern Lapwing in the rain, showing the effects of waterproofing with water beading on its back. This is an adult; its long crest and black from breast to face show it to be a male. Norfolk, UK, early April.

[Lower left] First-breeding Black Stilt. The total population of Black Stilts is only about 200–300 birds, all in New Zealand. There are two items of particular interest in this image. First, it shows how the flexibility of the upper mandible (rhynchokinesis) is exploited during preening. Note the gap between the mandibles mid-way along the bill, even though the bill tips are in contact; the bird has bent its upper mandible downwards. When shorebirds preen, the gap between the mandibles is generally very slight, and it is unusual to see this behaviour quite so clearly. The advantages of bill flexibility are obvious if you imagine preening with a pair of rigid chopsticks! Second, Black Stilts take about two years to reach maturity and acquire their completely black adult plumage. As juveniles they have white underparts, largely similar to other stilt species, which suggests that their ancestor was a pied-type stilt, and that the species has relatively recently evolved its all-black adult plumage. This stilt is about a year old and has black adult-type upperparts, but still has its juvenile brownish wing-coverts and extensive white underparts. South Island, New Zealand, mid November.

[Opposite] Adult Long-billed Curlew, preening. Florida, USA, mid September.

[Upper left] Adult breeding Common Redshank, dipping its bill to acquire a drop of water to aid the preening process. Norfolk, UK, early April.

[Lower left] Adult breeding Common Redshank, continuing to preen after bill dipping. Common Redshanks, as with other *Tringa* species such as Common Greenshank, the two yellowlegs and Willet, often have a plumage when breeding that is a combination of dark, patterned, breeding-type upperpart feathers and plain non-breeding ones. Norfolk, UK, early April.

[Opposite] First non-breeding Wilson's Phalarope preening, showing the amazing contortions that shorebirds can make to preen all those difficult-to-reach nooks and crannies! Northern Chile, mid November.

Ruff and Curlew Sandpiper, the males either do not show a preen oil compositional change (Ruff) or the compositional change occurs more frequently in the female than in the male (Curlew Sandpiper). Exactly the same occurs with Mallard ducks *Anas platyrhynchos*, where it is only the female that incubates and she has a preen oil compositional shift that does not occur in the drake.

WING STRETCHING

Wing stretching is an important part of plumage maintenance. It is usually done either with both wings raised together, which is often referred to as 'wing-lifting', or with one wing spread sideways, usually while standing on one leg with the other stretched sideways as if to support the wing and with the tail fanned sideways. Alternatively, both wings may sometimes be stretched sideways and given a good shake! All these actions help straighten and realign misplaced wing feathers, and may be done either during preening or even briefly while the bird is feeding, ensuring that its wing feathers are properly aligned and that the bird is ready for immediate flight should this become necessary.

HEAD SCRATCHING

Head scratching is another integral part of the preening process. The shorter billed birds can use their bills to preen all but their heads, which they preen by scratching with their feet; longer billed birds need to use their feet to scratch their upper neck as well. All bird species use one or other of two methods to scratch their heads: standing on one leg, they use the other foot to either scratch their head directly with the wing remaining folded, or they lower the wing on the side of the scratching foot and scratch with the leg held over the inner wing but under the outer wing. The two methods are known as 'direct' (or underwing) scratching and 'indirect' (or overwing) scratching, respectively. It is not known why or how these different head-scratching techniques have evolved, but each shorebird family consistently uses either one method or the other.

The various shorebird families – Magellanic Plover, oyster-catchers, Ibisbill, stilts and avocets, lapwings and the plovers – are all indirect head-scratchers, while the thick-knees, painted-snipe,

[Upper left] Adult New Zealand Dotterel (race *aquilonius*), wing-stretching, which serves to reposition displaced flight feathers. Wing-stretching is a stylised action in shorebirds, the wing often appearing to be supported by the corresponding leg which is stretched below it, while the tail is fanned towards the stretched wing. This bird is moulting out of breeding plumage, gaining the paler non-breeding underpart feathers, and has just started to renew its inner primaries, with one (dark) new feather at the bend of the wing, the others growing, but still retaining most of its older (browner) outer primaries; North Island, New Zealand, mid January.

[Lower left] Juvenile 'Western' Willet (race *inornata*) wing-stretching. Although it may have lost one or two of its buff-brown juvenile scapulars, it has yet to grow any of the grey first non-breeding feathers. The striking black-and-white wing pattern cannot be seen when the wing remains folded. Florida, USA, mid September.

[Above] First non-breeding Surfbird, wing-stretching. Surfbirds have rather plump toes, the soles of which are 'padded'. This is an adaptation to enable them to maintain their footing on the wet rocks where they spend most of their lives. It has replaced its juvenile upperparts with brown-edged grey non-breeding feathers, but the remainder of its plumage is juvenile. California, USA, early November.

Adult Variable Oystercatcher, showing the silvery-grey undersides to its flight feathers. As with wing-stretching, wing-lifting ensures that the wing feathers are correctly aligned. North Island, New Zealand, early November.

[Opposite] Adult breeding Bar-tailed Godwit, wing lifting. Probably of the nominate race *lapponica*, it has recently returned to its non-breeding grounds after breeding in northern Scandinavia or north-western Russia. It is regaining the non-breeding pinkish bill-base, but has not yet commenced either wing or body moult. Norfolk, UK, late July.

Head Scratching. Shorebirds use two different styles of head-scratching as part of their preening behaviour: 'indirect' (with wing lowered) and 'direct' (with wing remaining folded). These images show examples of both methods, illustrating how the more closely related genera use similar head-scratching methods. The oystercatchers, stilts and avocets, lapwings and plovers use the indirect method, while the sandpipers use the direct method.

[Right] Adult Chatham Oystercatcher head-scratching indirectly. This is another of New Zealand's and the world's rarest shorebirds that only occurs on the Chatham Islands, east of South Island, New Zealand. Chatham Islands, late November.

[Middle] Adult Southern Lapwing (race *fretensis*) head-scratching indirectly. Argentina, late November.

[Below] European Golden Plover head-scratching indirectly while bathing. An adult female, based on the lack of black on the face. The males of this northern form have extensive black on the face. Iceland, late June.

[Left] Adult breeding Diademed Sandpiper-plover, head-scratching indirectly. Despite its double-barrelled name, this behaviour clearly shows that its affinities are with the plovers, not the sandpipers. It had been ringed when a full-grown juvenile in February the year before the photo was taken; the month following the photo it was seen with a seven day-old chick. Northern Chile, late November.

[Middle] Adult Marbled Godwit, head-scratching directly. Florida, USA, mid September.

[Below] Sanderling, head-scratching directly. First-breeding, aged by the worn, retained juvenile wing-coverts that contrast with the more recently acquired and less worn non-breeding grey upperparts. Norfolk, UK, early April.

[Opposite] Adult non-breeding Long-billed Dowitcher, head scratching directly. It is showing rhynchokinesis, flexing the tip of its upper mandible upwards, and is closing its eye to avoid possible damage from its claws. It has just lost a tiny feather, which can be seen immediately below the raised foot. California, USA, late November.

Shorebirds with webbed and palmate feet.

[Above] Adult Pied Avocet, feeding while swimming in relatively deep water. It appeared to be searching quite deeply, presumably at the water–mud interface, and was thrusting very vigorously with its webbed feet to aid this process. This feeding behaviour is very similar to that of a feeding dabbling duck. The colour rings showed that it was at least 13 years old when photographed, about 5 km from where it had been ringed. Later sightings by other observers showed that it subsequently reached an age of at least 21 years. Norfolk, UK, early April.

jacanas, woodcocks and snipe, the sandpipers (dowitchers, godwits, curlews, *Tringa* species and phalaropes), coursers and pratincoles, all head-scratch directly.

SHOREBIRD PHYSIOLOGY

The physiological aspects of feeding, particularly those associated with the mechanics of the bill, have already been discussed in Chapter 3. Here, various other aspects of shorebird physiology are dealt with.

WEBBED FEET?

Webbed feet are more usually associated with wildfowl than with shorebirds. In wildfowl, the feet are entirely webbed, and the webs span the complete area between the three front-pointing toes. It is clear that in this case the purpose of the webbed feet is for swimming. Unlike wildfowl, many shorebirds have no significant webbing, although some have restricted webbing or 'palmations'. A few species have lobed feet, similar to the lobed toes of coots and related species, while a small number of other species have almost completely webbed feet. This variability poses some interesting questions.

The two most obvious reasons for shorebirds to possess webbed or palmate feet are either as an aid to swimming or to improve the bird's stability and mobility when walking on soft sediment. In the case of the species that have partial webbing, the extent of webbing is always greater between the outer and middle toes than between the middle and inner toes. This applies whether the webbing is between all three toes or just between the outer two; the reason for this is presumably to improve stability when walking on soft surfaces by increasing the effective spacing between the two feet, thus widening the walking platform. The only shorebirds that possess extensive webbing comparable to that of wildfowl are the Banded Stilt and the avocets, while those species with partial or restricted webbing between all three toes include the North American species Semipalmated Plover, Semipalmated and Western Sandpipers, and Stilt Sandpiper. Nordmann's Greenshank also has palmations

[Above] Adult breeding male Northern Pintail *Anas acuta*. This attractive dabbling duck frequently feeds in a very similar manner to the Pied Avocet, driving with its webbed feet to reach food items at the water–sediment interface. Norfolk, UK, early March.

[Upper right] Common Ringed Plover, showing the minor palmation that it has between its outer toes only. Adult breeding male, nominate race *hiaticula*. Sutherland, UK, mid June.

[Lower right] Semipalmated Plover differs from the closely related Common Ringed Plover in that it has palmations between all three front toes; this image shows the diagnostic webbing between the centre and inner toe (compare with Common Ringed Plover, upper right). Adult female, Florida, USA, late May.

First non-breeding Short-billed Dowitcher. This species has a significant palmation between the outer toes, virtually none between the inner toes. The 'tiger-striped' wing-coverts and tertials are diagnostic of this species at this age; the plain upperpart feathers are newly acquired non-breeding feathers. Florida, USA, mid November.

between all three toes, the only *Tringa* species that has, as does the closely related Terek Sandpiper. Intriguingly, the Eurasian Common Ringed Plover, which is closely related to the North American Semipalmated Plover, has very reduced palmations – only between the centre and outer toes – compared to the Semipalmated Plover.

Similarly, minor palmations between the outer and centre toes only are possessed by the following: the oystercatchers; Crab Plover; Ibisbill; South American Painted-snipe (but not the two *Rostratula* painted-snipes); most if not all curlews (including Upland Sandpiper); Short- and Long-billed Dowitcher; all the *Tringa* species, including Common **and Spotted Redshanks**, Lesser Yellowlegs, Green, Solitary and Wood Sandpipers, Grey-tailed and Wandering Tattler, and Willet (which has slightly larger palmations as would be expected from its scientific name *Tringa semipalmata*); and also Common and Spotted Sandpipers. Wilson's Phalarope has lobed toes, while Red-necked and Grey/Red Phalaropes have both lobed toes and partial webbing. Again, the palmations between the outer and centre toes are larger. No other shorebird species have significant palmations, although a few (such as Grey Plover and Kentish Plover) do have vestigial webbing between the outer toes.

Another interesting adaptation is that possessed by the Surfbird of the rocky coasts of the North American Pacific, which does not have any palmations but instead has cushioned soles to its toes to improve its grip on wet rocks. The two turnstone species have a similar adaptation, but to a lesser extent than the Surfbird.

NO HIND TOE?

Some shorebird species not only lack palmations, but also lack a hind toe. This applies to all the thick-knees, to the stilts and to Sanderling, the only *Calidris* species to lack a hind toe, presumably an adaptation to their sandy beach water's edge fast-running feeding style.

SWIMMING

It is not surprising that the avocets and Banded Stilt that have well developed webbed feet swim regularly, as do the lobed and partially webbed phalaropes that spend so much time at sea when

[Upper] Common Redshank, which has small palmations between the outer toes only. When feeding this species regularly swims short distances if it encounters water too deep for wading, presumably taking advantage of the palmations. Adult in non-breeding plumage. Norfolk, UK, early March.

[Lower] Common Sandpiper; another shorebird with palmations only between the outer toes. Adult in breeding plumage. Sutherland, UK, early June.

[Upper left] Adult American Coot *Fulica americana*. As a genus, the coots have all developed lobed feet, presumably as an aid for swimming and walking on soft ground. The lobes are proportionally larger than those of phalaropes but, unlike phalaropes, coots are not palmate. California, USA, early November.

[Lower left] Adult male Red-necked Phalarope showing both palmations and lobed toes. Notice the fly on the wing-coverts, hitching a ride! Iceland, late June.

Shorebirds swimming. If necessary, most, if not all, shorebirds will swim, but very few species, apart from avocets and phalaropes, do so regularly. Here are some examples of shorebirds that only occasionally swim.

[Opposite] Grey Plover. This bird walked along the far side of the muddy channel, decided to cross to the near side, but found it too deep to wade so it swam briefly, partially opening its wings as it did so, exposing the species' diagnostic black axillaries. Grey Plovers have small palmations, but only between the outer toes, which no doubt aid the swimming process. Adult, non-breeding plumage. Norfolk, UK, early February.

[Left] Black-tailed Godwit. The water depth became too deep for wading, so this bird swam for a few metres. Black-tailed Godwits have no palmations, but can still swim! An adult in non-breeding plumage. Norfolk, UK, late October.

[Middle] Eurasian Curlew. The high tide meant that it needed to move, and for a short distance swimming was more energy efficient than flying. This species has small palmations between its centre and outer toes. Adult non-breeding. Cornwall, UK, mid September.

[Below] Wood Sandpiper. Another shorebird that is rarely seen swimming, although, as with all *Tringa*, it has small palmations between the outer toes. Adult, breeding plumage. Norfolk, UK, mid May.

[Opposite, upper right] American Oystercatcher, blinking its nictitating membrane, presumably either to moisten or clean its eye. The membrane is a transparent inner eyelid that is drawn from front to back across the eye. Adult female. Florida, USA, early January.

[Opposite, lower right] Eurasian Curlew, blinking its nictitating membrane. The relatively short bill suggests it is probably a male. Note the pink base to the bill of a non-breeding bird, compared to page 147, lower left. Cornwall, UK, mid September.

not breeding. Most other shorebird species will swim briefly if they have to, particularly if, while feeding, they encounter water that is too deep for wading. This includes species such as the Common Redshank whose small palmations between its toes presumably help improve its swimming efficiency.

THE NICTITATING MEMBRANE

All birds, shorebirds included, have a nictitating membrane that is effectively a third eyelid that lies behind the two main eyelids. It is partially transparent and is drawn horizontally across the eye, from front to back. Its purpose is probably to clean the eye and perhaps to provide protection from possible damage in situations where the bird still needs to retain some vision.

SPECIES WITH SPURS

The sheathbills, together with some species of lapwings and jacanas, have spurs – 'carpal spurs' – at the outer bend of the wing, which can be quite sharp in some lapwing and jacana species. The carpal spurs have a bony core and a horny sheath and, although they rarely seem to be used for fighting, they are an obvious element in threat displays when the wings are spread to expose them. In the case of the sheathbills and other lapwings and jacanas, the spur can be quite blunt – little more than a knob or patch of hardened skin hidden under the wing feathers. The species that have quite prominent spurs may show them when standing, although they are often hidden beneath the breast feathers and are perhaps best seen in flight. The lapwings with prominent spurs are Blacksmith, Spur-winged, River, White-crowned, Senegal, Masked and Southern Lapwings, together with the most lapwing-like of the plovers, the Pied Plover. Male lapwings have longer spurs than females. Of the jacanas, Pheasant-tailed, Northern and Wattled all have prominent carpal spurs.

TEMPERATURE REGULATION

Newly hatched shorebird chicks are unable to regulate their body temperature and need to be brooded by their parents, as described

Northern Lapwing, completely closing its nictitating membrane to protect its eye while head scratching indirectly, as do all lapwing species. An adult breeding female, as shown by the relatively short crest and the white feathering on its face. Norfolk, UK, late April.

Shorebirds with carpal spurs. Some lapwing and jacana species have sharp spurs at the bend of the wing, which seem to be primarily used in aggressive display and perhaps serve only as a weapon of last resort? The spurs are usually held hidden under the breast feathers and are often hard to see, except when the bird flies. Spurs average longer in males than females.

[Left] Adult White-crowned Lapwing showing its carpal spurs, which are particularly long and sharp in this species. Northern South Africa, mid November.

[Middle] Adult Masked Lapwings. Probably a pair, with the male being the further bird having the longer wattle and the visible black-tipped yellow spur. The (presumably shorter) spur on the nearer female is almost completely hidden. Race *novaehollandiae*, which colonised New Zealand from south-east Australia in the 1930s. South Island, New Zealand, late January.

[Below] Southern Lapwing, displaying its spurs. Adult, race *chilensis*. Peninsula Valdés, Argentina, late November.

Adult male Wattled Jacana raising its wings and exposing the spurs in threat display to a nearby bird. Venezuela, mid November.

The next four images show the difference in head shape resulting from the larger salt glands possessed by the more salt-tolerant of each of two species-pairs, giving Short-billed Dowitcher and Bar-tailed Godwit slightly steeper foreheads compared to Long-billed Dowitcher and Black-tailed Godwit. Both species-pairs are in similar plumages and were photographed at similar times of the year.

[Opposite, upper right] Adult non-breeding Short-billed Dowitcher. Slightly steeper forehead than Long-billed Dowitcher (below). Commencing moult to breeding plumage; the slight downward kink of the bill is a useful feature of Short-billed that aids separation from Long-billed Dowitcher. Florida, USA, early April.

[Opposite right] Adult non-breeding Long-billed Dowitcher. Commencing moult to breeding plumage. Florida, USA, late March.

in Chapter 5. In adults, energy losses can be minimised by reducing heat losses, which is the reason why shorebirds often roost with their bills tucked under their back feathers and stand on one leg with the other placed amongst the breast feathers.

SALT GLANDS

In the previous chapter it was pointed out that shorebirds are rarely seen drinking, and when they do it nearly always seems to be fresh water. This observation raises the question of how they deal with the salt they ingest when feeding, as many species must do when foraging in brackish or saline waters. The answer is that, as in many other birds particularly marine species, shorebirds have two salt glands that aid the excretion of salt. These glands are situated in the forehead in front of the eyes; their size is greatest in those species that regularly feed in marine or saline environments, particularly those (oystercatchers, for example) that consume the flesh of bivalves. The size of the salt glands varies not only with the usual feeding environment of the particular species (marine, brackish or fresh-water), but will also vary in the shorter term with individual birds, depending on, for example, the ambient temperature or whether or not the bird is actively migrating. Oystercatchers and Purple Sandpipers are largely coastal species that have proportionately large salt glands, as presumably do the phalaropes, particularly Red-necked and Grey, which spend more than half their year at sea. It is no surprise, therefore, that all these species have particularly steep foreheads.

The ingested salt circulates in the blood and is extracted and stored temporally by the salt glands, then excreted through the nostrils to run down the bill to drip from the tip. It seems likely that shorebirds are able to control when they discharge the excess salt, and do so when it does not inconvenience other behaviour. Discharging salt while preening, for example, would contaminate their plumage.

Closely related species that differ in their feeding environments, such as Long- and Short-billed Dowitchers and Black- and Bar-tailed Godwits, where the first of each species-pair prefers fresh-water and the second uses brackish or marine environments, differ

subtly in head shape. Although the differences are quite small, it is interesting to note that in both cases the species favouring the more saline habitats has the steeper forehead, and presumably has the larger salt glands.

REFERENCES

Gutiérrez, J.S., Dietz, M.W., Masero, J.A., Gill, R.E., Dekinga, A., Battley, P.F., Sánchez-Guzman, J.M. and Piersma, T., 2012. Functional ecology of saltglands in shorebirds: flexible responses to variable environmental conditions. *Functional Ecology*, **26**, 236–244.

Jehl, J.R., 1975. *Pluvianellus socialis*: biology, ecology, and relationships of an enigmatic Patagonian shorebird. *Transactions of the San Diego Society of Natural History* **18**, 25–73.

Reneerkens, J., Piersma, T. and Sinninghe Damsté, J.S., 2002. Sandpipers (Scolopacidae) switch from monoester to diester preen waxes during courtship and incubation, but why? *Proceedings of the Royal Society of London B* **269**, 2135–2139.

Simmons, K.E.L., 1987. The head-scratching method of the Ibisbill *Ibidorhyncha struthersi*. *Ibis* **129**, 114–115.

[Upper] Adult non-breeding Bar-tailed Godwit. Slightly steeper forehead than Black-tailed Godwit (lower). Norfolk, UK, early March.

[Lower] Adult non-breeding Black-tailed Godwit. Norfolk, UK, early March.

[Opposite] Adult Eurasian Curlew discharging salt. This curlew simply stood on the muddy foreshore with fluid discharging from its nostrils and dripping almost continuously from its bill. This continued for almost five minutes, when the flow appeared to cease and it resumed feeding. Norfolk, UK, late February.

5 / 'THIS IS MY PATCH'

SHOREBIRD BREEDING AND TERRITORIAL BEHAVIOUR

SHOREBIRD MATING SYSTEMS

Amongst the shorebirds there are a surprising variety of mating systems. These various systems are of interest in their own right, but also invite speculation as to how they may have evolved, and provide interesting background information on the reasons for the range of breeding plumages shown by the different species. For example, in species that are monogamous and where the sexes play similar or equal parts in the raising of the young, the male and female generally have similar breeding plumages, as with the two yellowleg species in North America, and Common Redshank and Common Greenshank in Europe and Asia. In contrast, species such as Eurasian Dotterel, the painted snipes and the phalaropes, all of which have 'reversed' sexual roles, also have reversed breeding plumages, with the females being the brighter.

Table 2 shows, in brief outline, the more important shorebird mating systems, together with an indication of the different species involved. It must be stressed that this is a simplification, for example Sanderlings that breed in arctic Canada use the rapid multi-clutch

system, whilst those breeding in Greenland show simple monogamy where both members of the pair play their usual roles.

The majority of shorebirds are monogamous, with both birds of the pair taking part in nest selection and nest building (which is rather rudimentary in most shorebirds), incubation and caring for the young once they have hatched. This is 'simple' monogamy. The 'rapid multi-clutch' system is a development of simple monogamy with a single pair of adults involved, but two clutches are laid in quick succession, the first of which is incubated by the male and the second by the female. This is made possible by the fact that chicks of nearly all shorebirds are able to feed for themselves almost immediately after they hatch, and the system is presumably an adaption that allows the maximum number of young to be reared in the short arctic summer when food is easily available. What is surprising is that this system is used by the Sanderlings in arctic Canada, but not by those breeding in Greenland, where climate and habitat must be very similar to those in Canada.

Polygyny occurs when a single male regularly mates with two or more females. There are three main forms: 'harem' or 'simultaneous' polygyny, where a male breeds simultaneously with several females (examples being White-rumped and Curlew Sandpipers), 'serial' or 'successive' polygyny, where a male mates with two or more females in succession (for example Eurasian Woodcock), and 'male dominance' or 'promiscuous' polygyny, in which a male mates with any available female, of which the best known example is the lekking behaviour of Ruffs. Although the males may mate with any available female, there is evidence with several of the lekking species that the females may individually select the males with which they mate. This is consistent with observations that despite juvenile Ruffs having a range of slightly different plumage patterns, it is not unusual to encounter small migrating groups of two or three juveniles with identical patterns, suggesting that all may have the same parents.

Polyandry involves individual females that mate with two or more different males. In one of the few examples of 'simultaneous' polyandry in shorebirds, female Northern Jacanas of Central America hold a territory large enough to support several males, each

Table 2. Simplified summary of the mating systems used by shorebirds.

Mating system			Examples
Monogamy		Simple	thick-knees, oystercatchers, stilts, avocets, lapwings, many plovers, seedsnipes, snipe, godwits, curlews, most *tringa*, many *calidrids*, coursers, pratincoles
		Rapid multi-clutch	Mountain Plover, Sanderling, Temminck's Stint, Little Stint
Polygamy	Polygyny	Harem or simultaneous	White-rumped Sandpiper, Curlew Sandpiper
		Serial or successive	Eurasian Woodcock
		Male dominance or promiscuous (some through lekking)	Great Snipe, Pectoral Sandpiper, Buff-breasted Sandpiper, Ruff
	Polyandry	Simultaneous	Northern Jacana
		Serial or successive	Eurasian Dotterel, painted-snipe, other jacanas, Spotted Sandpiper, phalaropes

Breeding behaviour of thick-knees. The Eurasian Stone-curlew is a protected species in the UK and the photographs were taken under licence.

[Right] Male Eurasian Stone-curlew. The nest is sited in a field that is about to be sown for carrots (note the neatly prepared beds in the field behind), but the nest site itself has been carefully left undisturbed. Two chicks – the usual number for Eurasian Stone-curlews – successfully hatched and had left the nest by the next morning. This male had been ringed nearby as a chick, eight years previously. Norfolk, UK, mid July.

175

[Upper left] Eurasian Stone-curlew nest, egg and recently hatched chick. The chick still has its small white egg-tooth at the tip of its upper mandible. The remaining egg started to hatch about six hours after this photograph was taken. Norfolk, UK, mid July.

[Lower left] Peruvian Thick-knee chicks. Note the similarity in the patterning of their downy plumage with the Eurasian Stone-curlew chick, upper left. Northern Chile, mid November.

[Upper right] Eurasian Stone-curlews changing over during incubation. The male, with prominent black borders to the white line across the folded wing, approached from behind and after a few moments the female (greyish lower border to white line on wing) got up, allowing the male to settle himself on the egg. The chick went walkabouts briefly, but quickly returned to be brooded. Norfolk, UK, mid July.

[Lower right] Pair of Peruvian Thick-knees, the parents of the two chicks as shown lower left. As with the Eurasian Stone-curlew, there are small differences between the adult plumages of the two sexes of most thick-knees, but apparently not with Peruvian Thick-knees! Northern Chile, mid November.

Breeding behaviour of oystercatchers.

[Above] Magellanic Oystercatcher. This is in several ways the most 'different' of all the oystercatcher species. It is the only one to have a combination of a yellow eye and a yellow orbital ring – all the other American species have a yellow eye, but a red orbital ring. It also has some curious, high pitched calls, different from the other oystercatchers. It is also different in its 'piping' display. As with all oystercatchers, the piping display may be given at any time of the year and, although it seems to be basically territorial, there may also be a male–female bonding element. The Magellanic Oystercatcher, uniquely amongst the oystercatchers, cocks up its tail when piping, as seen here. Tierra del Fuego, Argentina, early December.

[Upper left] American Oystercatcher, in piping display. A male (no black flecking on iris). Florida, USA, mid September.

[Upper right] Eurasian Oystercatchers in piping display. These two pairs (from left to right: pair one, male and female; pair two, female and male) are disputing their common territorial boundary, early in the breeding season. Norfolk, UK, late March.

[Middle, left and right] Eurasian Oystercatchers mating. Norfolk, UK, late April.

[Lower left] Eurasian Oystercatchers, pair. The differences between sexes when adult are similar in most oystercatcher species. The male (right) has a shorter bill that is proportionally deeper at mid length. The pupil appears nearly circular in males, but in the female it looks oval due to black flecking on the iris forward of the pupil. This pair have mated recently, but the male clearly didn't wipe his feet first! Norfolk, UK, mid April.

[Lower right] Eurasian Oystercatcher nest. Earlier clutches usually have three or four eggs; later in the season, as here, the clutches are often smaller. Four days later these two eggs had hatched. Many shorebirds that nest in the open decorate their nests, but they usually do so when incubating and the decoration is of material within easy reach of the nest, as were the mussel shells here. If there is no suitable decorative material nearby, the nest remains plain. Sutherland, UK, mid June.

of which individually and more-or-less simultaneously incubates a clutch and raises the young. Although the plumages of male and female Northern Jacanas are similar, the females (as with other jacanas) are substantially larger than the males, which enable them to dominate the males and to defend their territory against other females.

Eurasian Dotterel, together with painted-snipes, phalaropes and the other jacana species, practice 'serial' or 'successive' polyandry and lay several clutches in succession for different males to rear. Except for the jacanas, the females of these species all have brighter breeding plumage. The North American Spotted Sandpiper, which also practices serial polyandry, provides an interesting comparison with the remarkably similar and clearly closely related Common Sandpiper of Europe and Asia. The sexes of the monogamous Common Sandpiper have largely similar plumages year-round, but the Spotted Sandpiper has evolved a distinctive breeding plumage with heavily spotted underparts. It is usual for the female to have larger and more extensive spots, although the differences from the male can sometimes be subtle. Perhaps serial polyandry is a relatively recent adaptation in Spotted Sandpipers and, consequently, the females are still evolving a breeding plumage more obviously different from the males?

It is possible that at least some Spotted Redshanks practice polyandry as the females regularly commence southerly migration quite early, leaving the males to care for the chicks.

AGE OF FIRST BREEDING

The age at which shorebirds first breed, and consequently when they attain their first full breeding plumage, typically depends on size. The small species breed in their second calendar-year, while the larger species may not breed until their third calendar-year or even later. Most oystercatcher species do not breed until they are at least four years old, and are thus amongst the oldest species when they breed for the first time. Eurasian Oystercatchers, particularly, often have difficulty finding a breeding territory and consequently may be significantly older than four years before they finally breed.

[Upper left] Eurasian Oystercatcher chicks a short distance from the nest in page 178 about two days old. The younger (above) still retains its white egg tooth, but that of the slightly older bird has already been lost. Sutherland, UK, mid June.

[Upper right] American Oystercatcher chicks, about three days old. Note the slightly different patterns of the downy plumage of the American and Eurasian Oystercatcher chicks (see previous image). Florida, USA, mid May.

[Middle, left and right] When nesting, Eurasian Oystercatchers do their best to distract potential predators. This adult male flew, calling angrily, at the intruding photographer (the bird was further away than it appears!), and then landed and did its equivalent of the 'rodent-run' distraction display used by smaller shorebirds, with tail fanned downward, running with a crouched stance, low to the ground. Sutherland, UK, mid June.

[Lower left] Adult Eurasian Oystercatcher feeding chick. All oystercatcher species (as with a small number of other shorebird species) feed their young. This young chick (no more than two days old) has just had a worm placed in front of it by its parent, which it promptly consumed. This chick was one of two that spent most of their time out of sight amongst the boulders, only emerging when one or other of their parents flew in, calling and carrying a prey item. Sutherland, UK, mid June.

[Lower right] Adult male Eurasian Oystercatcher with full grown juvenile. Juveniles remain at least partly dependent on their parents for food for periods of several weeks to several months. This juvenile is probably a couple of months old and is still associating closely with is parent. The dirty face of the adult is a result of probing for food. The juvenile has browner plumage than the adult, with neat pale-fringed upperparts and wing-coverts, a dark tip to the bill, a dark eye and duller, paler legs. It will soon acquire the broad white fore-neck collar of its first non-breeding plumage. Cornwall, UK, late September.

[Above] Adult female and juvenile Variable Oystercatchers. As with other oystercatchers, juvenile Variable Oystercatchers remain dependent on their parents for food for significant periods. Both these birds are of the black morph; pied morphs have variable amounts of white on their underparts. The juvenile is of comparable age to that in opposite, lower right, and similarly has neat pale-fringed upperparts, wing-coverts, a dark tip to the bill, a dark eye and duller, paler legs. South Island, New Zealand, late January.

Banded Stilts breeding at Lake Ballard, Western Australia, in early April 1995. By the time these photographs were taken, just 40 days after Cyclone Bobby had dumped about a third of a metre of rain in four days, 20,000 breeding pairs of stilts had found the flooded site, attained full breeding plumage, laid their eggs and hatching had commenced. Very few people have had the good fortune to experience the excitement of an active Banded Stilt breeding colony; by fortunate coincidence I happened to be in Western Australia when this breeding colony was discovered. The accompanying photographs give some indication of one of the wonders of the shorebird world.

[Above] The normally dry, flat salt lake was about a metre deep when these photographs were taken. Abandoned eggs can be seen at the near side of the colony. At the time of writing (2016) there had not been another Banded Stilt breeding event at Lake Ballard, which emphasises their irregularity.

[Upper left] Adult Banded Stilt on nest, brooding a newly hatched chick and three eggs. The broad, dark-chestnut breast-band that gives the species its English name is only worn when breeding and is acquired amazingly quickly, within days. The eggs are larger than those of other stilts and hatch a couple of days earlier, both being adaptations that enable them to breed quickly to exploit the brief periods when conditions are suitable.

[Lower left] Once the young have hatched, the parents escort the chicks through the colony, where they are likely to get prodded if they wander too close to adult birds still incubating their eggs. The striking white downy plumage of the chicks is unique for a shorebird, and they are the only species of stilt that has webbed feet, allowing them to swim readily.

[Upper right] Having reached the lake, the white-plumaged chicks rapidly group into crèches under the guidance of a few adults, the white plumage enabling lost chicks to quickly find another crèche and regroup.

Aspects of the breeding behaviour of Pied Avocets.

[Above] Adult female Pied Avocet (with the slightly more upturned bill) soliciting copulation from the slightly larger male (longer, slightly straighter bill), who feigns indifference as he preens, before mounting the female. Norfolk, UK, late June.

[Opposite] After mating, the male (left) dismounts and momentarily – and rather charmingly – holds his spread wing over the female. Norfolk, UK, early April.

DISPLAYS

OPEN HABITAT SPECIES – OYSTERCATCHERS, LAPWINGS AND PLOVERS

Worldwide, the noisy, piping behaviour of all the oystercatcher species must be one of the most familiar displays of all shorebirds. Given year-round by single birds or in groups of up to seven or more, with head raised and bill held downwards, they give 'kewit' calls that accelerate to a trill, then slowly die away, only to abruptly start again. In the non-breeding season, the piping display seems to be given primarily to establish dominance when feeding. When breeding, it is used most often when there is a territorial boundary dispute between adjacent pairs. One explanation of the display is that it is stylised aggression that has evolved to avoid the physical injuries that might otherwise be inflicted by the oystercatchers' robust bills. As the piping display is used by all oystercatcher species, it must be of considerable antiquity, inherited from some common ancestor species.

The breeding behaviour of lapwings and plovers is typical of many shorebirds that breed in open habitats. Of the lapwing species, the most well-studied, particularly in terms of behaviour, is the widespread Northern Lapwing of Europe. In the non-breeding season, they can be seen feeding in loose flocks in grassland and on arable, with flock size varying from a few birds to 1,000 or more. From time to time there are aggressive interactions, when one bird attempts to feed too close to another; a chase or fight will ensue, with the looser flying off to feed elsewhere, usually towards the margins of the flock. Occasionally two will display to one another in the 'high upright' pose, head up and tail down, with the wings sufficiently open to display the breast-band. They walk side-by-side while doing this and then turn to face one another, at which point the intensity of the display increases, with the tail being dropped and the wings opened further. Males will also display in this way to one another when breeding, and it seems likely that it is the males that do this in the feeding flocks.

In the breeding season, the feeding ground territorial displays are largely replaced by spectacular display flights, visible from some distance. These display flights are given by individual males and include a sequence of 'pee-wit' and similar song elements; however,

early in the breeding season while territories are being established, two or more males may be involved in the flights and aggression may occur.

Once the territory is established, and the male has attracted a mate, the nest scrape display that is an important part of the breeding cycle of many shorebirds, commences. The male tilts forward, breast to the ground, while scraping with alternate legs, tail held high, displaying his orange-chestnut undertail-coverts to the female, who initially stands behind him appearing disinterested, but then moves to the scrape hollow to repeat the display just given by the male. In both lapwing and other plover species the male may make a number of such scrapes, in one of which the eggs are eventually laid.

SHOREBIRDS THAT NEST AMONGST VEGETATION

The widespread Common Redshank of Europe and Asia is another shorebird species whose breeding behaviour is quite well known. Indeed, there are many parallels with the behaviour of Northern Lapwings. The first signs of Common Redshank breeding activity is typically in mid March when males start their graceful but noisy display flights. After a steep ascent from the ground which takes them to about 50 m (165 feet), the wings are spread and held slightly bowed, and they rise and fall, giving a yodelling '… teeoo, teeoo, teeoo, teeoo …' almost continuously, sometimes for two or three minutes, while flying over a considerable area. All this is to attract a female. Having done so, the display ritual is continued on the ground, when the male chases the female, head held low, tail spread. Particularly in the early stages of courtship these chases may end with aggression from the pursued female. This behaviour was once interpreted as territorial clashes between presumed males because it is impossible to distinguish males from females, but observations of colour-ringed birds have shown that both male and female are involved. Territorial fighting between males probably does occur, although later in the breeding season when it can be quite vigorous.

A fairly frequent element of Common Redshank display is 'wing-lifting', when both wings are raised showing the strikingly

Pied Avocets at nest. Most shorebirds, including the Pied Avocet, lay a clutch of three or four eggs. In the UK the Pied Avocet is legally protected from disturbance when breeding. Here, the nest site has been fenced off and was photographed from outside the protected area. The nesting bird can be seen as a small white dot above and to the left of the sign. Norfolk, UK, late June.

[Top] The female, while incubating her four eggs, is picking up small pebbles in an attempt to 'decorate' her nest. As all the pebbles in the area are very similar, not much was achieved, but in another location she might have been able to be more selective. Norfolk, UK, late June. A few moments later [middle] the male approached her from behind and they did a 'change over': she (right) got up, allowing the four eggs to be seen (note the slightly straighter and longer bill of the male, left) and [below] he sat down to continue the incubation. Norfolk, UK, late June.

[Upper left and upper right] Adult male Pied Avocets showing aggressive territorial behaviour when breeding. This behaviour occurs close to their nest site, and aggression is shown to other shorebirds (as with the Eurasian Oystercatcher here) and to other bird species, as well as to their own species. Since adult Pied Avocets can easily move some distance from the nest to feed, and thus do not need to defend the area close to the nest as a feeding area for themselves, it seems likely that the site is being protected from other avocets as a potential feeding area for newly hatched chicks or from other species that are perceived as a threat to eggs or chicks. Norfolk, UK, late April and mid May respectively.

[Lower left and lower right] Avocet chicks, as with most other shorebirds, leave the nest on hatching, and are accompanied by both parents. Here [left] the chicks (about two to three days old) are being cared for by the female (bill more strongly upturned) – two chicks exploring, whilst one is brooded. [Right] The same three chicks about 15 minutes later are accompanied by the male (straighter bill) as they swim from the immediate area of the nest. Norfolk, UK, late May.

white underwings that are visible from some distance. The male will subsequently make a number of nest scrapes, exposing an area of bare soil, lowering his breast to the ground, rotating his body and scratching backwards with his feet. This usually occurs amongst clumps of grass or similar vegetation and is therefore less frequently observed than with the similar display given by lapwings and small plovers that nest in more open situations. One of the nest scrapes is eventually selected for egg laying. Copulation is usually preceded by the male wing-lifting behind the female, and then the female will adopt and remain in a horizontal position while the male approaches her, calling loudly, standing tall and vibrating his raised wings before mounting.

Although many shorebirds will sing in display flight, some, such as the seedsnipes, sing from prominent positions in their breeding territories.

LEKKING BEHAVIOUR

Only three shorebird species use a lek as part of their mate selection: Great Snipe, Buff-breasted Sandpiper and Ruff. The lek is a relatively small area at which several males will display. In the case of the Ruff, it is usually on slightly raised ground where the males will be conspicuous. In all three species, once mating is completed the males play no further part in raising the young and leave the females unattended to nest, incubate the eggs and care for the chicks. Unlike the Ruff, the other two species are not dimorphic in size or plumage. There are three types of breeding male Ruff: 'resident' males, which defend their individual small territory within the lek, have dark ruffs and are slightly larger; 'satellite' males have pale ruffs, are slightly smaller and, as their name suggests, frequent the periphery of the lek and are not territorial; and 'faeder' males (from old English for 'father'), which are smaller (although larger than the females) and have female-type plumage. The faeders are only a very small proportion of the males at the lek and have only recently been recognised as males. Like the satellite males, their only chance to breed is through sneak matings with the females when the territorial males are otherwise engaged.

[Left] Two male Northern Lapwings in aerial display – and conflict – establishing their individual territories. Regularly giving their 'peewit' calls, these two continued their territorial dispute for over 20 minutes. It is unusual for lapwings to make physical contact (bottom). Males have longer inner primaries than females, giving their outer wing a more bulging rear profile, well shown in these images. Norfolk, UK, early April.

[Opposite] Two breeding male Northern Lapwings performing the 'high upright' territorial display. It is well into the breeding season, and one bird has just landed in the breeding territory of the other. After a few moments of low intensity display standing side-by-side, they turned to face each other and the intensity of the display increased as the tails were lowered and the wings spread slightly more. Then, after a moment or two staring at each other, the bird on the left flew off, presumably realising he was trespassing! They may also walk side-by-side in the low intensity display. Both these birds can be sexed as males by the continuous black area from bill to breast-band and by the relatively long crests; breeding females have white flecking below the bill and shorter crests. It is less easy to distinguish between the sexes early in the non-breeding season when adults of both sexes appear quite similar, but from about November those with the longest crests are males. Norfolk, UK, mid May.

[Upper left] Pair of breeding Northern Lapwings, male left, female right. The reeds have recently been cut, providing enough space for this pair to consider breeding. The male is making the nest-scrape display, breast in the scrape, presenting his orange-chestnut undertail covets to the female. He is deepening and extending the scrape, alternately with one foot and then the other. The female appears rather disinterested. [Below] A few minutes later the signs are more encouraging, as the female is now showing her interest by trying the scrape just made by the male. Norfolk, UK, late March.

[Opposite] Northern Lapwing with young. This female has four small chicks, perhaps three or four days old; the male is feeding not far away. Lapwing chicks, as with most shorebirds, feed themselves as soon as they leave the nest, but are attended by the adults. Periodically the female started calling, a quiet, mellow 'whooo-up', repeated every few seconds, and the chicks would come to be brooded as she squatted on her tarsi, pushing themselves into the shelter of her partly spread wings.

[Opposite, right] Female Northern Lapwing. She is calling to her chicks to come to be brooded. Some Northern Lapwings breed in their first summer, and this female is one of those; the worn and faded tips of the folded year-old juvenile primaries can clearly be seen. As well as worn primary tips, first-breeding females tend to have rather shorter crests and more white on the throat than older birds. Norfolk, UK, mid May.

[Opposite, middle] The female had been brooding all four young until this one emerged – only three then left in the shelter! Norfolk, UK, mid May.

[Opposite, below] Northern Lapwing chick. One of the chicks of the female, above, feeding by 'picking'. The white nape is conspicuous, probably aiding the adults to watch them. However, if the chick crouches in alarm the white area is largely obscured so as not to attract unwanted attention. The chicks of many of the lapwing species (and indeed many of the chicks of the smaller plovers) have a similar white nape collar, presumably for similar reasons. Norfolk, UK, mid May.

NESTS

The majority of shorebird species nest on the ground, either in the open or amongst short vegetation. Those nesting in open areas have the advantage that they can see potential predators from a distance and usually leave the nest cautiously when the predator is still at some distance away. In contrast, those species that nest amongst vegetation tend to sit much tighter and only leave the nest when the predator is quite close. The only hole-nester is the Crab Plover of the Middle East, whose underground nest helps with temperature regulation in this hot region. A small number of the *Tringa* species, such as Green, Solitary and Wood Sandpipers and Grey-tailed Tattler, may use old songbird nests from previous years, and the Nordmann's Greenshank may sometimes build its own twig nest in a tree.

Some open-area nesters decorate their nests with shells or other contrasting material (such as small animal droppings, twigs and grass stalks) which is collected, when available, from the immediate vicinity of the nest, usually by the sitting bird.

Another unusual nester, for a shorebird, is the Shore Plover of New Zealand, which nests under vegetation as a protection from predators. This strategy worked well when the Shore Plover's only predators were other bird species, but with the introduction of mammalian predators such as rats and cats to New Zealand, the Shore Plover was soon extirpated from everywhere except for a few small predator-free islands.

In most cases shorebirds nest close to their feeding areas, if only because the young need to feed almost as soon as they have hatched. Oystercatchers, which feed their young for some time after hatching, are an exception and may nest some distance from their feeding grounds.

CLUTCH SIZE

Most shorebirds lay a single clutch of four, perhaps three, eggs. If they lose their eggs, replacements may be laid later in the season when the clutch is usually smaller, perhaps only two or three eggs. Some species, such as the thick-knees, lay just two eggs, but the hole-nesting Crab Plover generally has only a single white egg, the usual egg colour of hole-nesting bird species. Other shorebird

eggs are all coloured, with random darker markings, and are laid at approximately daily intervals usually early in the morning. Incubation commences only when the clutch is complete.

EGG COVERING

Egg covering is a behavioural trait shown by a number of bird species, including non-shorebirds such as grebes, which use nest material for this purpose. The reason for egg covering is probably to help hide the eggs from the attentions of predators and, in hotter climates, to shelter the eggs from the direct rays of the sun and thus help maintain optimal incubation temperatures. Amongst the shorebirds that have been recorded covering their eggs with sand or soil are Little Ringed Plover, Kittlitz's Plover, White-fronted Plover, Kentish Plover, Egyptian Plover (which may also wet its eggs to cool them) and Three-banded Courser. Egyptian Plovers' eggs may hatch when covered and the chicks themselves may be buried by the parents if danger threatens. The use by shorebirds of nest material, as opposed to soil, to cover eggs has apparently only been recorded for the seedsnipes.

The Three-banded Courser of eastern and southern Africa actually incubates with its eggs almost completely buried, and because the nest is usually in a shaded situation it seems likely that the reason for burying the eggs is at least partly to disguise the eggs.

NEST AND CHICK DEFENCE DISPLAYS

Many shorebirds use quite elaborate anti-predator displays in an attempt to distract predators from their nest sites or from their young. The larger species often use a 'broken-wing' display, while the smaller species indulge in the 'rodent-run'. In both displays the bird crouches close to the ground, either spreading one or both wings as if it is injured, or runs from the predator in a manner reminiscent of a small rodent. Usually the display takes the bird away from the nest site or its chicks and eventually it flies off, or it may lift and wave a wing as if to indicate where it is – suggesting a broken wing – and invite further pursuit. Usually it seems to be the male that does the display, although often with the female close by.

Larger species, such as oystercatchers, may dive at predators – including intruding humans. As with terns, they call loudly at

[Upper left and right] Common Ringed Plovers giving the nest-scrape display. Initially the male is nest scraping, just as the male Northern Lapwing on page 192, with the female close by. Then the female comes up behind him to try out the scrape for size. Note the less black head pattern of the female compared to the male. Norfolk, UK, late March.

[Lower left and right] Male Common Ringed Plover giving predator distraction display.

[Lower left] Many small shorebirds will do a 'rodent-run' display to distract potential predators from their nest or chicks, calling continuously while doing so. With Common Ringed Plovers it usually seems to be the male that displays, although often with the female in fairly close proximity. It is difficult to get a photograph of a bird side-on when its preference is to run away! Sutherland, UK, mid June.

[Lower right] When they get a sufficient distance away from the nest area they then give the 'broken-wing' display. There were several Common Ringed Plover nest-scrapes nearby that day, none (that could be found) with eggs, although three days later one scrape had a single egg. Sutherland, UK, mid June.

[Opposite] Common Ringed Plover nest, showing how inconspicuous they are, in spite of nesting in the open. Most of the larger pebbles have been moved while nest-scraping, but one remains as a surrogate egg! Norfolk, UK, late July.

[Right] Common Ringed Plover chick. As with many other lapwing and small plover chicks it has a conspicuous white collar that must help the parents keep an eye on it. This chick was exactly ten days old when photographed. Norfolk, UK, early August.

[Middle] Shore Plovers in pre-copulation display, coastal North Island, New Zealand. They are two of the tiny number of one of New Zealand's highly endangered shorebird species, from a population introduced to nearby Mana Island, just north of Wellington. This island had been cleared of mice in 1990 as part of a general restoration plan to make the island safe for possible introductions. Unfortunately, the pair had chosen a very public and potentially hazardous mainland breeding site. Both were about one-year old, the male (right) having been hatched in captivity, whilst the female was reared by birds introduced to Mana Island. They nested about two weeks after this photograph was taken and they (and their single egg) were transferred to the captive population at New Zealand's National Wildlife Centre to minimize the risk of the birds or egg being predated. Apparently a single rat had arrived on Mana Island that eventually killed three-quarters of the introduced Shore Plovers, and caused the survivors to move to the adjacent mainland. Elsewhere, on the Chatham Islands (east of South Island) the populations are probably at equilibrium, and consequently do not normally breed until their second or third year. Although the Mana plovers were initially surprisingly successful, the introduction attempt has, sadly, now been abandoned. North Island, New Zealand, mid-November.

[Below] This is the very public bit of coastline that the Shore Plovers in the previous photograph had chosen for breeding. This species is unusual in nesting under vegetation, their nest site being under the bush on the right. Mana Island is in the background, about a couple of kilometres away. North Island, New Zealand, late November.

[Above] Mating Madagascan Jacanas, the female soliciting copulation in a very similar manner to many other shorebirds. The female is immature and has still to develop the white hind-neck of a full adult that is possessed by the male. Madagascar, early December.

[Opposite] Singing male Grey-breasted Seedsnipe of the race *orbignyianus*. During the breeding season the males sing from prominent song posts, giving a sustained, monotonous dove-like 'pu-ku, pu-ku'. Central Chile, late November.

the potential predator, but unlike terns, which can sometimes be frighteningly aggressive, they rarely if ever approach very closely, but pull away at some distance. Oystercatchers attacking in this manner usually land, still calling loudly, and do their less dramatic version of the rodent-run, with body held low and tail lowered, running away from the nest or chicks. Sometimes they may also perform a broken-wing display or they may feign incubation, sitting on an imaginary nest. Interestingly, the Ibisbill, which is relatively closely related to oystercatchers, responds similarly to potential predators once it has chicks, although before then its behaviour is much more cautious. With Common Ringed Plovers the rodent-run display may be seen during the nest-scrape stage before any eggs have been laid.

Species that nest semi-colonially, and at relatively high densities, may mount a cooperative defence against aggressors. Pied Avocets, for example, will take flight in numbers to mob Marsh Harriers, calling loudly as they do so.

HATCHING

Most shorebird clutches hatch more-or-less synchronously, although perhaps over a period of several hours, after an incubation period usually between 18 to 30 days depending on species and location. Clutches laid by smaller species generally hatch more quickly than those of larger species, and those of arctic species usually hatch more quickly than comparable temperate or tropical species. The chicks break out of the egg aided by an egg tooth, a small but sharp projection at the tip of the upper mandible, which is lost soon after hatching. On hatching they already have their downy plumage, which dries quickly, and they are able to leave the nest, although they will not do so until all the chicks have hatched. In some cases, the adults may brood them in the nest for a while, perhaps over their first night. At this stage the chicks of most species are able to feed themselves, but because they are initially unable to regulate their body temperature, brooding by the adults, mainly by the female in monogamous species, is a regular event both during the day and at night. The extent of brooding depends on the weather conditions, particularly the temperature, and on the age of the chicks, becoming less frequent as they get older.

Shortly after hatching most shorebird species will lead their chicks to feeding areas, sometimes travelling quite substantial distances. Newly hatched shorebirds retain egg yolk in their stomachs for several days, which they use to supplement their food requirements during their early life.

Sheathbills are exceptional because the young hatch asynchronously over several days and then stay in the nest for about a month, where they are brooded continuously for the first two weeks, and then with lesser intensity. The first chicks to hatch grow faster and have higher survival rates.

FEEDING YOUNG

Some shorebirds do feed their chicks, although the length of time for which they do so varies with species. Those that feed young for a few days include the thick-knees, Egyptian Plover and the polyandrous painted-snipes, whose chicks are fed only by the male. Woodcocks and snipe may feed earth worms to their young, again for just a few days, although the chicks find much of their own food. Coursers and pratincoles show similar behaviour, but the food items for these species are usually insects.

A few species, however, feed their young for much more than just a few days. Sheathbills, reflecting their asynchronous hatching strategy described above, feed their chicks for up to two months. The Magellanic Plover feeds its young with food carried to them in its crop (the only shorebird to do so), apparently at least until they fledge, probably longer. The chicks of most oystercatcher species remain dependent on their parents for food for a period of time, depending on the type of food available. Those feeding on annelid worms, which the young can catch almost as easily as the adults, may become independent after a few weeks. In contrast, those feeding primarily on bivalves or crabs, which the young need time to learn to handle, have a dependence period that may extend to several months. Small worms and crabs are placed on the ground in front of the chick or the chicks may compete for worms dangling from a parent's bill – the more successful chicks grow at a greater rate than their siblings. The size difference between chicks can be obvious only a few days after hatching. The atypical hole-nesting

[Upper left] Common Snipes of the race *faeroeensis*, presumably in pre-copulatory display described in *The Birds of the Western Palearctic* as: 'birds circle round each other, strutting, dropping wings, and cocking and fanning tails'. Copulation did not ensue on this occasion. Iceland, late June.

[Upper right] Common Snipe calling from prominent perch. When calling, the bill is only opened slightly, but note the distended throat. Cambridgeshire, UK, early June.

[Lower left] Common Snipe drumming. A number of the *Gallinago* snipe have a territorial display of this type, carried out in a roughly circular, switch-back flight, the drumming occurring when diving. The drumming – a curious goat-like bleating – is the result of the vibration of the single, spread outer tail feathers on each side of the tail. The North American Wilson's Snipe extends its outer two tail feathers when drumming. Northern Poland, late April.

[Lower right] Male Black-tailed Godwit (race *islandica*) calling in the rain, probably to alert its young to the presence of a potential predator. The wonderful orange base to the bill is a feature of its breeding condition. Iceland, late June.

[Upper left] Adult male Common Redshank in song flight. On coastal salt-marshes from March onwards, one of the first signs – and sounds – of breeding activity is the extensive song flight of the male. For as long as two to three minutes, flying at heights of up to 50 metres with wings slightly drooped and rapidly fluttered, barred tail spread, he calls continuously and circles a wide area trying to catch the attention of an unmated female. Norfolk, UK, early May.

[Upper right] Adult male Common Redshank in song flight. This is the view of the male that the female on the ground will have – the redshank's unique broad white area at the rear of the wing and its spread, barred tail are both clearly shown. Norfolk, UK, late March.

[Lower left and right] Once the male Common Redshank has attracted a potential mate the courtship continues on the ground, with the male (nearer) chasing the female. Male and female Common Redshanks are identical, and until research was carried out with colour-ringed birds of known sex this behaviour was interpreted as males in territorial dispute, the confusion being compounded as the female may respond aggressively to the male. In this case it is presumed that the more strongly marked, nearer bird, is the male. Norfolk, UK, late March.

Crab Plover usually has just a single chick, which, on hatching, is initially unable to walk and therefore stays in the nest hole where it is fed for a considerable period, initially on a pulp of crab meat and later on whole crabs.

COLONIAL BREEDING – BANDED STILTS

Only two of the world's shorebird species can truly be said to breed colonially: Crab-plover, whose colonies may have up to 1,500 nests (although usually fewer), and the Banded Stilt of Australia, whose largest recorded colony was one found after it had been deserted, with an estimated 179,000 nests.

Banded Stilts are an Australian endemic shorebird that, when not breeding, occur in large flocks at coastal saline lagoons. They breed irregularly at very remote ephemeral inland salt lakes and until recently surprisingly little was known of their breeding biology. Only a small number of breeding colonies (probably less than 30) have ever been discovered – the first in 1930. Many were found long after the colony had been abandoned, and all that remained were empty nests, scattered unhatched eggs and a few long-dead chicks.

Australia's salt lakes are usually dry, but occasionally – by no means every year – a cyclonic storm fills one of the lakes. This results in a hatch of brine shrimps that provides food in abundance for both adult and young Banded Stilts. Within days of a storm the stilts seem to know that there is a breeding site awaiting them, and they leave their usual coastal non-breeding sites, even though it may not have rained there. One such event occurred at Lake Ballard in Western Australia following the arrival of Cyclone Bobby in February 1995. It was suspected that the stilts might attempt to breed and a systematic aerial search was instigated that resulted in the discovery of two or three possible breeding colonies. One colony, on a small island in the now flooded Lake Ballard, already had nests and eggs, just twelve days after the cyclone! Amazingly, although there was little or no rain in the stilts' coastal non-breeding areas, the birds had moved about 1,000 km inland to exploit the potential breeding habitat provided by the newly flooded lake. This was a particularly exciting discovery because a stilt colony had not been found previously at such an early stage in the breeding cycle.

[Upper left] Common Redshanks in pre-copulation display. The female (this one is particularly poorly marked, both above and below) is stationary, soliciting copulation, body held horizontally, while the (much more strongly marked) male approaches from behind her, calling and standing tall, with wings spread and vibrating. Norfolk, UK, mid May.

[Middle left and opposite] Adult Common Redshanks fighting. Although some fighting occurs between individual males and females during courtship, it is likely that males fight for territorial reasons, as seems to be the case here. The length of time (over two minutes) and intensity of the fighting, well out in a shallow lagoon, is difficult to interpret as pair bonding! Norfolk, UK, mid May.

[Lower left] Nest of Common Redshank. A typical nest of this species, partly concealed within the vegetation. Kent, UK, mid May.

When flooded, Lake Ballard is dotted with small islands, offering protection from predators. A Banded Stilt breeding colony is best compared with a tern colony because both are noisy and full of action. Stilt colonies can be very much larger than tern colonies, and the one at Lake Ballard held an estimated 20,000 pairs at its peak. More recently, a colony discovered in 2010 at Lake Torrens, South Australia, held an estimated 140,000 birds.

The large numbers of birds at such a colony no doubt help to stimulate and synchronise breeding, so much so that at Lake Ballard the first chicks were seen on 3 April, just 33 days after the end of the principal rainfall event. Banded Stilt eggs are quite large (about 55 × 40 mm compared to 44 × 31 mm for the similar-sized Australasian Pied Stilt) and hatch more quickly than those of most other large shorebirds, presumably an adaptation to the short period when brine shrimps are available and also to the need to breed quickly as an anti-predator response. Clutch size is usually three or four, rarely two or five. The Lake Ballard colony showed that the incubation period is probably 20–23 days compared to 22–25 days for the Australasian Pied Stilt.

Shortly after hatching the parents lead the chicks to water, where the chicks gather in crèches accompanied by a few adults and feed largely on brine shrimps. Crèches of up to 1,400 chicks have been reported. The white plumage of the chicks, another Banded Stilt feature unique to shorebirds, possibly helps attract other chicks to the crèche. The chicks may move considerable distances from their natal site, particularly as the salt lake dries. On such occasions, chicks have been found wandering on main roads, often many tens of kilometres from where they were hatched.

There is much in common between Banded Stilts and flamingos in their breeding biology because both species share opportunistic communal breeding when conditions allow, have white-plumaged chicks and have young that show crèching behaviour (presumably aided by the high visibility of the chicks' white plumage). This is a notable example of convergent evolution.

At Lake Ballard there was very little predation of eggs or chicks, and although both crows and Wedge-tailed Eagles *Aquila audax* scavenged dead chicks, live chicks were only seen to be taken on two

[Left] Breeding plumages of male and female Spotted Sandpipers. Unlike the closely related Common Sandpiper of Europe and Asia, which is monogamous and has quite similar plumages year-round, the North American Spotted Sandpiper practices serial polyandry and has a distinctive breeding plumage with spotted underparts that gives the species its common name. The female (upper left) has the larger spots, and it is tempting to speculate that the plumage difference between the sexes, although slight, has evolved as with those of other species with the same mating system, such as Eurasian Dotterel and the phalaropes, whose females have brighter breeding plumages than the male. Both images Florida, USA, late August.

[Opposite] The three types of breeding male Ruff, the species well known for its polygynous breeding system. All three types play different roles at the lek.

[Opposite, upper left] 'Resident' males have dark ruffs and are strongly territorial within the lek. Northern Poland, late April.

[Opposite, upper right] 'Satellite' males have pale ruffs and play a peripheral role at the margins of the lek. It is presumed that the conspicuous pale ruff helps to attract the females' attention to the lek. Northern Poland, late April.

[Opposite, lower left] 'Faeder' male, its plumage (but not its structure) imitating that of a breeding female. I was in Cyprus, photographing a group of migrating female Ruffs when I was puzzled by one bird, closely similar in plumage to the typical females but marginally larger, whose proportions, with a rather small head compared to its body, suggested a male rather than a female. Puzzled, I took just five images and then forgot about it until, a couple of months later, I encountered a reference whose title referred to 'female mimics in a lekking shorebird'. My problem was solved – it had just been discovered that there was a third type of male Ruff, which the authors of the paper had named 'faeder', effectively a male Ruff in drag! Cyprus, late April.

[Opposite, lower right] Adult female Ruff in breeding plumage, for comparison with the 'faeder' male. The female has a less bulky body than the faeder, so that the faeder has a proportionally smaller head, although the plumages are quite similar. Cyprus, late April.

Three-banded (Heuglin's) Courser. With their large eyes, the four species of *Rhinoptilus* coursers are all largely nocturnal feeders. Three-banded Courser is notable for largely burying its eggs. The nest site is in the shade and, in the warm northern South African climate, burying the eggs probably maintains them at about the correct temperature for incubation. South Africa, mid November.

or three occasions. Elsewhere, however, Banded Stilt colonies have been heavily predated by Silver Gulls *Larus navaehollandiae*.

REFERENCES

Bom, R.A. and al-Nasrallah, K., 2015. Counts and breeding biology of Crab Plovers *Dromas ardeola* on Bubiyan Islands, Kuwait, in 2012–2014. *Wader Study* **123**, 212–220.

Campbell, B. and Lack, E., 1985. *A Dictionary of Birds.* T. & A.D. Poyser: Calton, UK.

Chandler, R.J., 1995. Salt lake stilt city. *BBC Wildlife*, December, 34–37.

Cramp, S. and Simmons, K.E.L. (eds.), 1983. *The Birds of the Western Palearctic*, III, *Waders to Gulls*. Oxford.

del Hoyo, J., Elliott, A. and Sargatel, J. (eds.), 1996. *Handbook of the Birds of the World. Volume 3: Hoatzin to Auks.* Lynx Editions: Barcelona.

Dowding, J.E. and O'Connor, S.M., 2013. Reducing the risk of extinction of a globally threatened shorebird: translocations of the New Zealand shore plover (*Thinornis novaeseelandiae*), 1990–2012. *Notornis* **60**, 70–84.

Ens, B.J. and Goss-Custard, J.D., 1986. Piping as a display of dominance by wintering Oystercatchers *Haematopus ostralegus*. *Ibis* **128**, 382–391.

Hale, W.G., 1980. *Waders.* Collins: London.

Hale, W.G., 1988. *The Redshank.* Shire Publications: Princes Risborough, UK.

Howell, T.R., 1979. The breeding biology of the Egyptian Plover *Pluvianus aegyptius*. The University of California publications in zoology, volume 113. University of California Press: Berkeley, CA.

Jukema, J. and Piersma, T., 2006. Permanent female mimics in a lekking shorebird. *Biology Letters* **2**, 161–164. doi:10.1098/rsbl.2005.0416

Minton, C., Pearson, G. and Lane, J., 1995. History in the mating: Banded Stilts do it again. *Wingspan* **5** (2), 13–15.

Nethersole-Thompson, D., 1988. *The Oystercatcher.* Shire Publications: Princes Risborough, UK.

Pienkowski, M.W. and Green, G.H., 1976. Breeding biology of Sanderlings in north-west Greenland. *British Birds* **69**, 165–177.

Shrubb, M., 2007. *The Lapwing.* T. & A.D. Poyser: Calton, UK.

Simmons, K.E.L., 1961a. Foot-movements in plovers and other birds. *British Birds* **54**, 34–39.

Simmons, K.E.L., 1961b. Further observations on foot-movements in plovers and other birds. *British Birds* **54**, 418–422.

6 / 'IN AUGUST, GO HE MUST'

SHOREBIRD MIGRATION

The final two stanzas of a traditional English rhyme about the Eurasian Cuckoo are:

'… in July he prepares to fly, in August go he must'.

These phrases also apply to the migration of Arctic breeding shorebirds. Indeed, we now know that there are a number of parallels between cuckoos and shorebirds, not least that both make continuous, long-distance migratory flights lasting several days, and that shorebird migration, like that of the adult Cuckoo, commences in late June or early July, and is well underway by August.

The majority of the world's long-distance migratory shorebirds breed in the northern hemisphere and migrate south for the northern winter, with some species moving well south of the equator. This allows them to take advantage of the abundant northern summer food supply in the breeding season, and then move back south when the summer food supply diminishes. This can be regarded as a 'standard North–South migration'. Unsurprisingly, there are many variations on this theme, from short distance movements of little more than a hundred kilometres or so, some of which may perhaps be better described as 'Seasonal Movements', to long distance flights of several thousands of kilometres. The terms 'hop', 'skip' and 'jump' have been used to categorise different types of migration, particularly northward movements on the return to the breeding grounds. Examples are the relatively short distance 'hops' made by Ruddy Turnstones, the longer distance 'skip' movements made by Dunlins, Common Redshanks and, as has recently been shown, by Temminck's Stints. Examples of long-distance 'jump' flights are those made by Great Snipe, Bar-tailed Godwits and Red Knots and, in the southern hemisphere, by a significant proportion of New Zealand's population of Double-banded Plovers.

'Leapfrog' migration is practiced by a number of the northern shorebird species. A good example is Common Ringed Plover, of which races *psammodromus* (breeds in arctic Canada, Greenland and Iceland) and *tundrae* (breeds in northern Scandinavia and eastwards to northern Russia and eastern Siberia) both leapfrog over western Europe where the nominate race *hiaticula* is largely sedentary. The two migratory races spend the northern winter as far south as west Africa (both races) or even South Africa (*tundrae*). Other northern hemisphere migrants that have a similar leapfrog migration strategy include Bar-tailed Godwit and Common Redshank.

In contrast to the situation in the northern hemisphere, no species of shorebird breeding in the southern hemisphere migrates to the northern hemisphere after breeding. Indeed, only a handful of shorebirds undertake long-distance migration within the southern hemisphere, including the Brown-chested Lapwing, Double-banded Plover and Madagascar Pratincole. The Brown-chested Lapwing breeds in west Africa during December–May and migrates east to spend July–December in the Victoria basin of east Africa. The majority of the population of Double-banded Plovers breeding inland on New Zealand's South Island move across the Tasman Sea to spend the Austral winter in eastern and south-eastern Australia. Madagascan Pratincoles move northwest across the western Indian Ocean from Madagascar to spend their non-breeding season in coastal east Africa.

Northbound migration.

Adult breeding Bar-tailed Godwits, male left, female (long bill) right. The smaller, more distant and out-of-focus birds are Great Knots. On mud flats at low tide, along the Yellow Sea (west) coast of South Korea. The female carries a white flag, indicating that she is from New Zealand, one of the population of the race *baueri* that makes the longest migration of any shorebird species, moving north to stage at the Yellow Sea where they remain for four to five weeks to refuel, before departing to Alaska to breed. The bulging undertail profiles of both birds shows that they have put on substantial fat reserves for the next leg of their migration. Females of race *baueri* can weigh in excess of 500 g just prior to migration, a substantial gain on their non-breeding minimum of around 330 g; for the smaller males, the weights are 400 g compared to 270 g. South Korea, late May.

Bar-tailed Godwits leaving Broome, Western Australia, heading for the Yellow Sea. A late afternoon in early April; periodically one or two godwits flew up from the mud flats calling loudly, to be joined by others to form a group that circled upwards in loose formation, becoming a skein of as many as 250 birds that flew off towards the north, still calling. This was repeated several times with similar sized groups of godwits. The calling ceased, although there were still shorebirds on the mudflats, but the show seemed to be over. Then godwits could be seen returning to the mudflats in ones and twos. Over the next 10 to 15 minutes a significant proportion of the departing birds returned, although not in the confident groups that had departed earlier. That night there was a severe storm – did the birds hear the low frequency infrasound the storm generated ahead of them, and decide to postpone their departure?

MIGRATION STUDIES AND TECHNIQUES

Ringing (or banding) studies have long been used to provide data on bird migration and some of the current schemes have been running since the early 1900s. The use of metal rings (or bands) requires the ringed bird to be recovered in some manner (for example, by recapture or being found dead) so that the ring number can be read and reported. Alternatively, by using several colour rings in combination, or with colour rings or flags engraved with numbers or letters, sightings using binoculars or telescope allow the movements of individual birds to be tracked. Photography can allow a ring number to be read from an image or series of images.

More recently, increasing electronic miniaturisation has allowed the use of three different tracking techniques, depending on the size of the bird. The first uses global positioning system (GPS) tags, with which larger shorebirds can be equipped, enabling their movements to be followed more-or-less in real-time. The second approach involves Platform Transmitter Terminals (PPT), which are the most recent development in tracking devices and are effectively less sophisticated GPS devices. They are lightweight (about 5 g) and solar-powered, and have been successfully deployed on Eurasian Cuckoos *Cuculus canorus* in the UK, and on medium-sized shorebirds, such as Great Knots, in Australia. They are capable of more-or-less real-time location data to an accuracy of 500 m, sufficient for most ornithological purposes.

The third technique is the use of light-level geolocators. These devices simultaneously record time and light level, which, in combination, enable the bird's position to be determined. The disadvantage is that geolocators require the bird to be re-trapped so that the tag can be retrieved and the stored data downloaded. The advantage is that their small size and weight (about a gram) allows them to be used on even the smallest shorebirds. All three of these techniques enable the actual routes taken by individual birds to be mapped and, as a consequence, our understanding of shorebird migration is advancing rapidly.

FINDING THE WAY - NAVIGATION METHODS

Migrating shorebirds are impressively good navigators, even on

[Left] Adult breeding Bar-tailed Godwits departing from the Yellow Sea for their Alaskan breeding grounds. After circling around to gain height, they formed into a 'V' and disappeared towards the north. Two days later, virtually all the staging godwits had gone, together with most of the other shorebirds, and the mudflats were practically deserted. South Korea, late May.

[Middle] Common Greenshanks are a relatively common migrant shorebird along all the European–African–Asian–Australasian flyways, although they seem to be more numerous and to travel in larger groups in the east, particularly on the East Asia/Australasia flyway, as here. This group has just been disturbed by the rising tide and is presumably flying to a roost site. South Korea, late April.

[Below] Dunlins (most with the black belly of breeding plumage) and a Short-billed Dowitcher (centre, also in breeding plumage). Both species may have spent the non-breeding period in the area where they were photographed or (particularly the dowitcher) they may have spent some time further south. Having acquired breeding plumage, they are either about to start the journey north or are pausing briefly having already commenced northward migration towards their Canadian breeding grounds. Florida, USA, early May.

their first migration – but how do they do it? The answer will not be covered in detail, but a few 'pointers' may not be out of place. Research over many years, largely with passerines rather than shorebirds, has shown that migrating birds use the equivalent of both a map and a compass, and it is generally assumed that what has been discovered about passerines also applies to shorebirds. On their first migration the 'map' relies on inherited instinct, but thereafter experience quickly fills in much detail, enabling the birds to revisit stopover locations on successive locations, as well as to return to successful wintering sites.

Birds have at least four 'compass equivalents' that are used to maintain the correct flight direction. One, they have the ability to detect the inclination of the geo-magnetic field, which is near vertical at the magnetic poles and horizontal close to the equator, enabling birds to fly north or south providing they are aware of which hemisphere they are in. Two, if it is not cloudy, they can use their internal clock in combination with the sun's position. Three, when the sun is low, even if it is cloudy, sunlight polarised by the atmosphere provides orientation information. Four, at night guidance is provided by the stars, as the birds are able to identify the centre of celestial rotation – the Pole Star in the northern hemisphere – and use that as their reference point. It is probably no coincidence that most long-distance migrants commence migration in late afternoon, when they have all these compass equivalents available to them in quite a short period.

Another navigational clue that migrants may use is low frequency infrasound, which is generated by wind over mountain ranges or can perhaps warn of bad weather ahead.

SOME MIGRATION CASE STUDIES

LATHAM'S SNIPE

A recent geolocator study has provided details of the migration strategy used by Latham's Snipe, a species that breeds in Japan and far-eastern Russia in the northern summer and migrates south to eastern and south-eastern Australia when not breeding. A number of Latham's Snipe were fitted with geolocators in Victoria, Australia in October 2015, and one individual, 'TO', was recovered there just over a year later. The data downloaded from its geolocator showed that TO flew north towards the end of the Austral summer in February 2016, spent a couple of months in south-east Queensland, then paused on Cape York Peninsula (north-east Australia), from where it flew directly to Hokkaido, Japan, arriving in early May. In late August 2016, after presumably breeding, it returned directly to south-east Queensland, flying non-stop for three days. A month later it was back in Victoria, where the geolocators had been fitted a year earlier. This is a dramatic example of 'standard North–South migration' and shows that individual shorebirds can be amazingly site faithful, returning to areas with which they are already familiar from previous years.

GREAT SNIPE MIGRATION – HIGH SPEED OVERLAND

Another outstanding example of 'standard North–South migration' is shown by the Great Snipe, again revealed by geolocators. In a recent Swedish study, a total of 70 male Great Snipes were caught and tagged at their breeding-season leks, 19 of which were subsequently retrapped at the same site. The downloaded data from these birds demonstrated that two somewhat different migration strategies were used when returning to their non-breeding areas in sub-Saharan Africa. One group of birds departed from the breeding area relatively early, and made stopovers in northern Europe, before making a non-stop trans-Saharan flight averaging 4,700 km in around 54 hours. The second group dispensed with the stopovers, making a direct flight averaging 5,900 km from the breeding area to south of the Sahara, in about 68 hours. Both groups flew at average speeds of about 90 km/hour.

All made a stopover of about three weeks just south of the Sahara, before moving on to their non-breeding grounds in west and central Africa, close to the equator. After remaining there for about seven months, most departed in mid April and were back on their Swedish breeding grounds in mid May. The return flight involved an initial non-stop trans-Sarahan flight to south-east Europe, followed by a series of short flights and stopovers. Prior to this study virtually

[Opposite] Red Knots. From their location these are of the North American race *rufa*. Red Knots of this race migrate as far south as Argentina when not breeding. These are very bulky in the undertail area and have put on considerable fat reserves for the next leg of their journey northwards. The proportional mass increase is comparable to the *baueri* godwits page 210, if not greater. Florida, USA, mid May.

nothing was known of Great Snipe migration and its non-breeding strategy, and there was no indication that they made fast, non-stop flights as long as 6,000 km. These are also the highest average speeds so far reported for any species of long-distance migratory bird.

BAR-TAILED GODWITS – LONG-DISTANCE RECORD HOLDERS

The most spectacular long-distance 'jump' migration of all bird species so far recorded is made by Bar-tailed Godwits of race *baueri*, which breed in Alaska and then migrate south to spend the non-breeding season in New Zealand. Prior to migration they take on fuel in the form of fat, approximately doubling their body weight, and at the same time their organs that are not needed during flight, such as the gizzard and intestines, shrink substantially. Commencing in March, they migrate north-west across the Pacific, via the Yellow Sea, where they rest and re-fuel before continuing on to their breeding grounds in Alaska. After breeding, they return, if all goes well, in one flight direct to New Zealand.

Bar-tailed Godwit E7, a female, was fitted with a GPS transmitter in New Zealand in early February 2007, when she was also equipped with a black plastic 'flag', engraved 'E7' in white characters, on her upper leg. After release, E7 remained for a few weeks in the Firth of Thames, a major estuary just east of Auckland, North Island, putting on weight before departing northwards on migration on 17 March 2007. She flew continuously for about seven days and by 24 March she had reached the coast of China in the far north-west of the Yellow Sea, a distance of almost 10,000 km. She remained there for over five weeks to refuel, and then on 2 May flew east, then turned north-east, to reach the southern tip of Alaska on 8 May, flying a total distance of 6,500 km. She then made a few shorter flights still moving northward, another 700 km, reaching her presumed breeding area on 15 May. The total distance she had flown from New Zealand was about 17,500 km!

On 18 July, just over nine weeks later during which she was presumably breeding, she moved to the Yukon Delta in south-west of Alaska. There she spent the next six weeks, slightly longer than she had spent refuelling on the Yellow Sea on her northward migration. On 29 August she set off again, this time flying southwards until

[Above] Horseshoe Crab *Limulus polyphemus*. A very important stop-over site in eastern North America for American Red Knots on the northbound migration is Delaware Bay, where Horseshoe Crabs previously used to spawn in large numbers, their eggs providing a vital food-source for Red Knots and other shorebird species. Sadly, over-harvesting the crabs has reduced the food availability for the Red Knots and led to a significant population decline in the *rufa* sub-species. This is the shell of a dead crab; it is about 45 cm (18 in) from head to tail tip. USA, late October.

[Opposite] Grey Plovers. All except one bird have the black underparts of breeding plumage that give the species its American name 'Black-bellied Plover'. Note that the black body feathers in this plumage merge with the equally black axillaries at the base of the underwing, which are a feature of the species year-round (see also page 165). The exception (bottom right) is in non-breeding plumage but still has the signature black axillaries of this species, and is probably a second calendar-year bird that will not breed for another year. Females of this species regularly migrate further south than males, particularly those on the East Asia–Australasia flyway, where almost all those reaching Australia are females. South Korea, late May.

Adult breeding female Spotted Redshank. Female Spotted Redshanks migrate south from their breeding grounds before the males, who remain to care for the young. The females are therefore amongst the first shorebirds to be seen on return migration in western Europe. This individual was ringed on its southward migration in The Netherlands on 2 July 2008 when it was already adult (and was thus at least two years old). It was then re-sighted in Norfolk, UK, on 1 July 2013 and again at the same location on 27 June 2016, when this photo as taken. An example of faithfulness to a particular stop-over site. Breeding males are entirely black, but females, like this individual that is now a little worn at the end of the breeding season, have white streaking on the head and neck, extensive white tips to the underpart feathers, and much white on the undertail coverts. The ring is upside-down, and so the patience of the observer who read the number with a telescope in 2013 is to be admired – it is much easier to read on a series of photographs! Norfolk, UK, late June.

Southbound migration.

A flock of nine Whimbrels (with decurved bills) and three Bar-tailed Godwits. All are juveniles (note the neat, fresh plumage on both species and the lack of coloured breeding plumage on the godwits), making the first of their annual southward migration along the East Atlantic flyway. The Whimbrels will spend the northern hemisphere winter coastally anywhere from the Iberian Peninsula and south to west Africa, but the godwits may either remain where they were photographed or they could also move south as far as west Africa, depending on the race involved. Norfolk, UK, mid August.

close to Hawaii, then turning south-west to pass close to Fiji, to eventually make landfall on the Firth of Thames, New Zealand, late on 7 September, after a continuous flight of nearly 12,000 km in about nine days.

There had been suspicions that *baueri* Bar-tailed Godwits could make impressively long and surprisingly fast flights based on such evidence as leg-flag sightings, radar observations and the knowledge that there are very few suitable stopover sites, particularly south of the Yellow Sea. The direct evidence provided by E7's GPS transmitter provided confirmation and perhaps the most exciting result in animal migration studies yet recorded. At the time of writing it remains as the world record for a long-distance, non-stop flight. On the three legs of her annual migration, E7 flew at average speeds between 50 and 60 km/hr.

It is easy to presume that this was an unusual event relating to a single bird, but as Bar-tailed Godwits usually migrate in significant flocks, E7's achievement is repeated many thousands of times each year. Of course, each year many birds will be affected by bad weather and unfavourable winds, but E7 has shown what is possible, and very likely typical of *baueri* godwit migration when weather conditions are reasonably favourable. It even seems likely that their behaviour has evolved to take advantage of the assistance of northerly winds during their single-leg return flight.

A roosting shorebird will often tuck its bill and a leg into their plumage to conserve heat and thus energy (Chapter 7). This observation suggests that the longer legged species may similarly save energy on their migration flights by folding their legs into their underparts.

RED KNOT MIGRATION IN THE AMERICAS

A story that complements that of the Bar-tailed Godwit unfolded along the Western Atlantic Flyway (see later) in 2010. Red Knots of the American race *rufa* spend the northern winter in South America, some as far south as the southern tip at Tierra del Fuego. A number of these were fitted with geolocators in May 2009 while on their northbound migration to Delaware Bay, eastern USA. One year later three of these birds were recaptured on their return to Delaware Bay.

Bar-tailed Godwits, of two different races. The bird on the left (nominate race *L. l. lapponica*) having bred in Scandinavia or north-western Russia probably returned here to its non-breeding area four weeks or more ago, and has already largely moulted into its grey non-breeding plumage. The bird on the right, which is of the race *L. l. taymyrensis*, is still on migration and is still largely in breeding plumage. It not only bred later than the *lapponica*, but it has also flown considerably further, from the Taymyr peninsula in Siberia, and will probably not moult to non-breeding plumage until it reaches west Africa, where it will winter. Race *taymyrensis* has a moult and breeding schedule that is about a month later than that of *lapponica*. It provides an example of 'leapfrog' migration, breeding further north and east and wintering further south than *lapponica*. The *taymyrensis* individual is no longer in breeding condition because its bill now has a pink base rather than the completely black bill that (as a male) it would have had when breeding. It has also acquired a few grey non-breeding upperpart feathers. Norfolk, UK, late August.

The downloaded geolocator data showed that in 2009 they initially flew north-west to James Bay in the south of Hudson Bay, and then, after either breeding or simply wandering without breeding, all three migrated back south, two making significant detours when over the Atlantic to avoid tropical storms. One flew 5,400 km in six days, from Hudson Bay across the Atlantic to the Lesser Antilles, where it stayed a few days, and then moved further south in flights of up to three days, with intermediate stops, to winter in northern Patagonia, Argentina. The other two both wintered in northern Brazil. The bird that wintered in Patagonia returned in steps to Brazil, and then made a direct flight north over South America to the coast of North Carolina, USA, a distance of 8,000 km in 6 days. From there it returned to Delaware Bay. The geolocator of one of the Brazil wintering birds failed in Brazil, but the other bird on its return journey flew from Brazil direct to Delaware Bay, a distance of 6,700 km in 6 days.

In this case the use of geolocators demonstrated that a much smaller shorebird species could make long, continuous, flights of up to 8 days, rather surprisingly without stopping to refuel, and at speeds between 40–55 km/hour. The total distances flown on migration, assuming that they followed great circle routes, were between 17,500 km and 27,000 km. Given the smaller size of the Red Knots, this is every bit as much an achievement as the trans-Pacific flights of the Bar-tailed Godwits.

MIGRATION OF RED-NECKED PHALAROPES

Another surprising discovery, again with the use of geolocators, concerns the Red-necked Phalaropes that breed in Shetland, north of mainland Scotland. Of nine birds fitted with geolocators in 2012, just one, a male, was recaptured when it returned to Shetland the following year. The downloaded data showed that from Shetland it moved west across the Atlantic to the Labrador Sea off eastern Canada (taking six days), then moved south to Florida, USA, west again across the Gulf of Mexico to the Pacific, reaching an area between the Galapagos Islands and South America in mid October, where it stayed until mid April 2013. Then it retraced its outward migration route to return to Shetland, although its battery failed

Juvenile Eurasian Curlew. Ringed in Finland in early July, about 2,000 km north-east of where it was photographed. When it was ringed it was described as 'young, out of the nest', in other words it was still a chick. Now, about eight weeks later, it is fully grown and well into its southward migration. Eurasian Curlews ringed in the UK and Ireland have been recorded as far south as Iberia, where this one might be going. Norfolk, late August.

while it was still in the Atlantic. Until this extraordinary journey, 22,000 km in total, it had always been assumed that northern European Red-necked Phalaropes spent the non-breeding season in the Arabian Sea, and that the non-breeding birds in the Pacific were from the north American population. It now seems likely that, as well as the Scottish Red-necked Phalaropes, Icelandic Red-necked Phalaropes also move to the Pacific. A similar study of Swedish Red-necked Phalaropes has shown that they do indeed move as originally thought – in relatively short skips – to the Arabian Sea.

OTHER ASPECTS OF SHOREBIRD MIGRATION

The distances migrated by some shorebird species varies with sex, with females often, but not always, moving further south than males. Examples include Grey Plover, particularly those that spend their non-breeding season in Australia, almost all of which have been proven with DNA analyses to be females. Rather similarly, female Ruffs often migrate further south than the males, as far as sub-Saharan Africa, where they outnumber the males by about 10:1.

It is not clear why female Grey Plovers predominate in Australia, although perhaps males prefer to remain closer to their breeding grounds, ready for a rapid return in the spring so they can set up a breeding territory before the females arrive back. A similar explanation can be suggested for the difference in the sex ratio of the non-breeding Ruffs in Africa. Male Ruffs migrate back to their breeding grounds in April–May, a week or so earlier than the females, presumably to establish their position in the lek prior to the arrival of the females. The differing sex ratio when not breeding will also reduce competition for food resources, and the smaller size of the female Ruffs may perhaps be an adaptation to wintering in the warmer African climate.

In other shorebird species it is the males that move the greater distances, one example being the Bar-tailed Godwit. The males are smaller in this species and have shorter bills, and may therefore be less tolerant of cold weather and of the greater depths to which prey species retreat in these conditions.

One of the many other fascinating aspects of shorebird migration revealed by ringing studies is the regular use by individual

[Upper right] Juvenile Black-tailed Godwits. These birds, the majority of a flock of about 20 southbound migrants, flew in to the estuary and immediately started to preen to ensure that their plumage was in good condition if they were suddenly disturbed and had to move on. Their neat, small feathered, pale-fringed plumage shows them to be juveniles, and the relatively bright rufous colouration identifies them as birds from Iceland, race *islandica*. The other European race, nominate *limosa*, breeds and migrates south at least a month earlier than *islandica*, and juvenile *limosa* is rarely, if ever, seen in the UK in these numbers. Cornwall, UK, mid September.

[Lower right] Juvenile Black-tailed Godwits. Seven minutes after the previous photograph – and some are still preening, others are feeding and one is even sleeping. Two hours later they had gone. Cornwall, UK, mid September.

[Opposite and above] Migrating European Golden Plovers. Large flocks of European Golden Plovers occur regularly at this site during the northern hemisphere winter, but usually they are just roosting birds. This flock was different. As with the Black-tailed Godwits (page 223), they arrived suddenly, about 800 of them, dropping from the sky. As soon as they landed many started drinking and bathing, with much frantic splashing, jumping and wing flapping to shake off excess moisture. This energetic behaviour lasted barely three minutes when, as if with an unheard or invisible signal, they all took off and continued their journey along the coast. From their behaviour, I guessed that these were migrants moving south, just arrived from northern England or even Scandinavia. Norfolk, UK, mid October.

Juvenile Lesser Yellowlegs (left) and juvenile Common Redshank. Migrant shorebirds sometimes go astray, particularly young birds in their first year. Thousands of shorebirds take a great-circle route from northern Canada out over the Atlantic to get to southern USA or even northern South America. If they encounter bad weather they can be blown east to western Europe, which presumably explains the presence of this Lesser Yellowlegs in south-west England. Its companion, the closely related Common Redshank of Europe and Asia, provides a rarely seen comparison of these two closely-related species, still largely in juvenile plumage (although they have both acquired some first non-breeding upperparts). Cornwall, UK, late September.

birds of the same stopover sites at about the same time in different years. Some of the photographs show examples of this with shorebirds whose history is known from repeated sightings of their coloured rings or flags.

SEASONAL, COLD WEATHER AND OTHER MOVEMENTS

Outside the breeding season, many shorebirds move to ensure that they have constant access to areas where food is easily available. Such movements are usually relatively short distance and less 'systematic' compared to true migration. Seasonal movements in the northern hemisphere are often made in response to cold weather by such species as Northern Lapwings and Common Ringed Plovers. Prolonged freezing conditions are especially problematic.

In the southern hemisphere somewhat similar movements are made in the Austral winter in New Zealand by the South Island Oystercatcher and the Wrybill, both of which move south to north from their South Island breeding areas to coastal North Island. These 'internal migrants' typically travel 800–1,000 km each way and most of the population of both species are involved. Those of the New Zealand Double-banded Plovers that do not migrate to Australia may make similar seasonal movements.

Elsewhere in the southern hemisphere, seasonal movements are made by inland species that move to the coast after breeding, as do White-fronted Plovers in southern Africa. Most of the Andean breeding species in southern South America, such as Andean Avocet, Andean Lapwing, the South American true snipes, as well as the seedsnipes, probably make similar movements, from high altitude to low altitude coastal areas at the end of their breeding season.

An unusual type of seasonal movement, indeed arguably true migration, again in the southern hemisphere is undertaken by some African Black Oystercatchers. Adult Black Oystercatchers are largely sedentary and confined to coastal South Africa, but each year about 40% of the juveniles, particularly those hatched on the west coast, move 1,500–2,000 km north in short hops to coastal Namibia and Angola, well north of the range of the adult birds. There they remain for two to three years, and then return to their natal area and adopt the sedentary lifestyle of adults. Presumably this behaviour has evolved to reduce competition between the immature and adult populations.

One of the best examples of cold weather seasonal movements are those made by Northern Lapwings, usually in December and January. Large south-westerly movements can occur, sometimes involving thousands of birds, that are particularly obvious in southern Britain and Ireland when frost or snow makes feeding difficult. Sometimes movements of this type coincide with strong easterly airflows across the Atlantic and give rise to sightings of Northern Lapwings in eastern Canada or the north-eastern United States. These sightings usually occur singly, perhaps annually in Newfoundland, but there have also been small invasions in the past, most recently at the end of 2012, when a few Northern Lapwings were seen in the north-eastern United States and south-eastern Canada.

THE SHOREBIRD FLYWAYS CONCEPT

'Flyway' is a convenient although rather generalised term used to describe a geographic region that supports a group of populations of migratory birds throughout their annual cycle. Different major flyways for shorebirds have been recognised worldwide. One scheme of flyways relates them broadly on a continental basis as follows:

The Americas – Eastern Pacific, Central, Western Atlantic

Eurasia to Africa – north and east Atlantic, Europe, west Asia and west Africa, central Asia to east/southern Africa

Central/east Asia to southern Asia/Australasia – central Asia to southern Asia, east Asia to Australasia

West Pacific – Russian Far East/Alaska to the Pacific islands

Flyways are not neat, tidy corridors along which shorebird migration takes place; however, they are a useful concept, not least as a tool for research and conservation.

[Opposite] Adult male Black-tailed Godwit, race *islandica*. This bird was ringed on the Tagus Estuary, Portugal (left leg: orange over green; right: orange over green flag, or "OG-OGflag"), in mid February 2007, when it was at least two years old. This is another migrating shorebird that was remarkably faithful to its staging and non-breeding sites, as it returned to the Tagus in November of each year from 2007 to 2013, spending up to four months there, before commencing its return journey. It was reported in Iceland twice, at the same location in the east of the island, in late April/early May 2008 and on exactly the same dates in 2014, when it was probably still on the final leg of its migration. It was seen on numerous occasions during both its northward and southward migrations, mostly in eastern England, particularly north Norfolk, but also in Cambridgeshire, Lincolnshire and Yorkshire, County Clare, Ireland (late April 2011), western Belgium (mid March 2013), and Argyll, Scotland (late April 2013). It staged regularly at Cley, Norfolk, particularly on southbound migration, where it was seen every year from 2007 to 2014, and where (presumably) each year it moulted to non-breeding plumage. The final sighting was in Cambridgeshire, not far from Cley, in early April 2015. I first saw (and photographed) it in late August 2007, and then again in 2011. As the photographs show, in 2011 when it arrived on 7th August, it was still in breeding plumage (top), but by 1st October (below) it had moulted to non-breeding, though it may still have been in wing moult. Norfolk, UK, early August and early October.

TWO CRITICAL FLYWAY STOPOVER SITES: THE YELLOW SEA AND DELAWARE BAY

In all the shorebird flyways it is possible to identify individual locations that are particularly important as migratory stopover sites and are used for refuelling. Worldwide, one of the most important of these is the Yellow Sea area, bounded by China and North and South Korea, situated in the East Asia/Australasia (EAA) Flyway. At the end of the twentieth century, as many as two million shorebirds passed through this region each year on northward migration, and about a million on southward migration. At this time, the Yellow Sea area supported more than 90% of the EAA populations of six different shorebird species and more than 30% of the populations of a further 18 species. Sadly, these numbers are diminishing rapidly as a consequence of coastal reclamation, particularly in China and South Korea. For example, the global population of Great Knots, one of the major users of the Yellow Sea particularly on northbound migration, was estimated to be about 380,000 individuals in 2006, but following the reclamation of the tidal flats at Saemanguem, South Korea, about 90,000 individuals disappeared from the area. Surveys elsewhere in South Korea, together with a decline of the same magnitude and timing on their non-breeding grounds in Australia, led to an estimate that the global population had fallen to 292,000–295,000 individuals by 2007.

Another critical stopover site is Delaware Bay on the east coast of the USA. This extensive bay is the final migration stopover site for most *rufa* Red Knots and also for other shorebird species such as Sanderlings and Ruddy Turnstones before they fly the final leg of their migration to their Arctic breeding grounds. Delaware Bay is the major spawning ground for the ancient Horseshoe Crab *Limulus polyphemus*, on whose eggs the Red Knot feed, enabling them to double their body weight. They need to do this to provide sufficient fuel for both the final leg of their migration and also to enable them to breed at the earliest opportunity, even though their final destination may be snow-covered when they arrive.

At the beginning of the 1980s some 100,000 to 150,000 Red Knots used Delaware Bay in May to refuel on the crabs' eggs but their numbers fell sharply, and by 2003 were down to only about 12,000–

15,000. Moreover, only a small proportion of these had attained a weight exceeding 180 g by late May, a weight that is presumed to be needed to enable them to complete their migration and breed successfully. The reason for the rapid reduction in numbers of Red Knots was that from the early 1990s the Horseshoe Crabs were being harvested as bait for eel, whelk and conch fishing, and by the late 1990s well over two million crabs were being caught each year along the mid-Atlantic Coast. This resulted in far fewer crabs' eggs being available to the Red Knots and other shorebirds. Restrictions to the crab harvest were introduced from 1998, resulting in fewer crabs being taken, but a significant increase in Red Knot numbers did not occur until 2009. The latest figures (2012–2015) show an encouraging increase to about 25,000, although this is still far from the numbers of the 1980s. Further problems occurred in 2012 when Hurricane Sandy stripped vast quantities of sand from the beaches and destroyed nearly three-quarters of the Horseshoe Crab breeding habitat. An emergency beach replenishment scheme appears to have been surprisingly successful, and the numbers of Red Knot have remained largely unchanged since 2012.

Adult female Pectoral Sandpiper. The vast majority of Pectoral Sandpipers, which breed in northern North America and eastern Siberia, migrate south through the Americas to southern South America. A few, like this individual, are non-breeding visitors to both Australia and New Zealand. North Island, New Zealand, mid January.

REFERENCES

Bamford, M., Watkins, D., Bancroft, W., Tischler, G. and Wahl, J., 2008. Migratory Shorebirds of the East Asian–Australasian Flyway: Population Estimates and Internationally Important Sites. Wetlands International – Oceania: Canberra, Australia.

Barter, M.A., 2002. Shorebirds of the Yellow Sea: Importance, threats and conservation status. Wetlands International Global Series 9, International Wader Studies 12, Canberra, Australia.

Boere, G.C. and Stroud, D.A., 2006. The flyway concept: what it is and what it isn't. In: G.C. Boere, C.A. Galbraith and D.A. Stroud (eds.), *Waterbirds around the World.* The Stationery Office: Edinburgh, UK, 40–47.

Duijns, S., Jukema, J., Spaans, B., van Horssen, P. and Piersma, T., 2012. Revisiting the proposed leap-frog migration of Bar-tailed Godwits along the East-Atlantic Flyway. *Ardea* **100**, 37–43.

Game and Wildlife Conservation Trust, 2016. Available at www.woodcockwatch.com

Gill, R.E., Tibbitts, T.L., Douglas, D.C., Handel, C.M., Mulcahy, D.M., Gottschalk, J.C., Warnock, N., McCaffery, B.J., Battley, P.F. and Piersma, T., 2009. Extreme endurance flights by landbirds crossing the Pacific Ocean: ecological corridor rather than barrier? *Proceedings of the Royal Society of London B* **276**, 447–457.

Hansen, B., Honan, J., Wilson, D., Chamberlain, R., Stewart, D. and Gould, L., 2016. Latham's Snipe migration. *Tattler* **41**, 14.

Higgins, P.J. and Davies, S.J.J.F. (eds.), 1996. *Handbook of Australian, New Zealand and Antarctic Birds. Volume 3: Snipe to Pigeons.* Oxford University Press: Melbourne.

Hockey, P.A.R., Leseberg, A. and Loewenthal, D., 2003. Dispersal and migration of juvenile African Black Oystercatchers *Haematopus moquini. Ibis* **145**, E114–E123.

Lindström, Å., Alerstam, T., Bahlenberg, P., Ekblom, R., Fox, J.W., Råghall, J. and Klaassen, R.H.G., 2016. The migration of the great snipe *Gallinago media*: intriguing variations on a grand theme. *Journal of Avian Biology* **47**, 321–334.

Lislevand, T. and Hahn, S., 2015. Skipping-type migration in a small Arctic wader, the Temminck's stint *Calidris temminckii. Journal of Avian Biology* **46**, 419–424.

Marchant, S. and Higgins, P.J. (eds.), 1993. *Handbook of Australian, New Zealand and Antarctic Birds, Volume 2: Raptors to Lapwings.* Oxford University Press: Melbourne.

McCaffery, B. and Gill, R.E. 2001. Bar-tailed Godwit (*Limosa lapponica*). In: A. Poole and F. Gill (eds.), *The Birds of North America,* No. 581. The Birds of North America: Philadelphia, PA, 1–36.

Newton, I., 2010. *Bird Migration.* HarperCollins: London.

Nils, L.J., Berger, J., Porter, R.R., Dey, A.D., Minton, C.D.T., Gonzalez, P.M., Baker, A.J., Fox, J.W. and Gordon, C., 2010. First results using light level geolocators to track Red Knots in the Western Hemisphere show rapid and long intercontinental flights and new details of migration pathways. *Wader Study Group Bulletin* **117**, 123–130.

Pierce, R., 1999. Regional patterns of migration in the Banded Dotterel (*Charadrius bicinctus bicinctus*). *Notornis* **46**, 101–122.

Piersma, T., 1988. Hop, skip, or jump? Constraints on migration of arctic waders by feeding, fattening and flight speed. *Wader Study Group Bulletin* **53**, 6–8.

Smith, M., Bolton, M., Okill, D.J., Summers, R.W., Ellis P., Liechti, F. and Wilson, J.D., 2016. Geolocator tagging reveals Pacific migration of Red-necked Phalarope *Phalaropus lobatus* breeding in Scotland. *Ibis* **156**, 870–873.

Urban, E.K., Fry, C.H. and Keith, S., 1986. *The Birds of Africa, Volume 2.* Academic Press, Cambridge, MA.

van Bemmelen, R.S.A., Hungar, J., Tulp, I. and Klaassen, R.H.G., 2015. First geolocator tracks of Swedish red-necked phalaropes reveal the Scandinavia–Arabian Sea connection. *Journal of Avian Biology* **46**, 295–303.

Warnock, N., McCaffery, B.J., Battley, P.F. and Piersma, T., 2009. Extreme endurance flights by landbirds crossing the Pacific Ocean: ecological corridor rather than barrier? *Proceedings of the Royal Society of London B* **276**, 447–457.

Wernham, C.V., Toms, M.P., Marchant, J.H., Clark, J.A., Siriwardena, G.M. and Baillie, S.R. (eds.), 2002. *The Migration Atlas: Movements of the Birds of Britain and Ireland.* T. & A.D. Poyser: Calton, UK.

Wetlands International, 2015. *Waterbird Population Estimates.* Available at wpe.wetlands.org

Woodley, K., 2009. *Godwits. Long-haul Champions.* Penguin Books: Rosedale, New Zealand.

7 / SAFETY IN NUMBERS

SHOREBIRD FLOCKING, ROOSTING AND PREDATOR AVOIDANCE

FLOCKING

Shorebirds flock for various reasons – the most obvious are to feed, when migrating, to roost and to help avoid predators. Flocking to feed has been partly discussed in Chapter 3 and flocking for migration in Chapter 6. Flocking for roosting, which has the added benefit of making available many pairs of eyes to spot potential predators, is described here, together with associated behaviour, such as loafing and resting.

The main suggestions that have been made are (1) that flocking in general provides protection from predators on the assumption that there is safety in numbers, while the likely benefits of communal roosts are (2) that the flock functions to provide access to feeding sites, presumably by following congeners to feeding sites when departing from the roost, and (3) that the birds can assess if the numbers present are greater than the food resources can support. In the third case, the assessment of numbers is perhaps made during the birds' elaborate pre-roost flights, or 'murmurations', although an alternative or additional reason for these flights is that they confuse potential predators.

PRE-ROOST FLIGHTS – 'MURMURATIONS'

Shorebirds make spectacular, coordinated pre-roost flights in tightly packed flocks, just as do Common Starlings *Sturnus vulgaris* when performing their murmurations. As with starlings, the swirling, dense clouds of shorebirds with their ever-changing shapes that give the impression of a single coordinated entity, rather than hundreds or thousands of individuals, are one of the wonders of the avian world. Other animal aggregations, such as mammal herds, shoals of fish and swarms of insects show similar coordinated behaviour. The same general explanation for this extraordinary behaviour no doubt applies to shorebirds as it does to starling murmurations.

Murmurations of starlings have been studied using 3D video techniques, and it seems likely that the mechanics of the communal flights of shorebirds are similar. It turns out that the commencement of a turning manoeuvre occurs locally with a few birds in the flock, and then spreads through the flock from one individual to another, doing so at a rate that is surprisingly constant with time. The rate at which the starlings transfer the manoeuvring information ranges from 10 to 20 m/s. The mechanism by which the information transfers is uncertain, but it seems most likely to be visual.

ROOSTING

The choice of a roost site for shorebirds is primarily one that provides some degree of shelter, and where there is little disturbance. Roosting flocks of shorebirds can vary in size between just a few birds to many thousands, the numbers depending on the species, their lifestyle and local conditions. The largest high-tide roosts are those composed of shorebirds that feed on tidal mud flats, and therefore have to roost at high tide; the roost size is generally largest at the highest tides when almost all of their potential feeding areas are covered with water.

The act of roosting is more-or-less synonymous with sleeping, even though shorebirds rarely seem to sleep soundly. Roosting shorebirds usually stand on one leg, with the other leg held in its breast feathers, and its head turned with its bill tucked into its scapulars. Even then, eyes are opened frequently. This roosting posture enables the bare parts to be insulated to minimise heat loss, and so reduce energy expenditure.

A large flock of Red Knot in coordinated flight, having been disturbed by the rising tide. Shorebirds are targeted by a number of species of raptor. Individual birds minimise their chances of being caught by joining a flock and taking part in these spectacular 'murmurations'. The tight mass of birds is presumed to confuse any potential predators. Roosting Eurasian Starlings show similar behaviour, to which the term murmuration was originally applied. The majority of these birds are either newly returned from their high arctic breeding grounds, or are staging briefly before they migrate further south. Norfolk, UK, mid August.

High-tide roosts. All these roosts are composed of either migrating or non-breeding birds. Breeding season roosts are generally quite small and are primarily composed of non-breeding birds.

[Above] Massed flock of Dunlins. These were coming in to roost; most if not all are migrants, probably of race *alpina*, on their way to arctic breeding grounds in Scandinavia or northern Russia, staging at this location. Norfolk, UK, mid May.

[Opposite, upper left] European Golden Plovers arriving at their daytime roost. The low early morning light makes it immediately apparent why they are called 'golden' plovers. Norfolk, UK, early December.

[Lower left] A large flock of Bar-tailed Godwits in the Firth of Thames, North Island, New Zealand, roosting at high tide. It is January and these are probably of the race *baueri*, which breed in Alaska. They leave New Zealand in late March to stage for four to five weeks in the Yellow Sea, and then move north again to reach their arctic breeding grounds in May. Mid January.

[Upper right] Black-tailed Godwits. These are birds of the race *islandica*, which breed in Iceland as their name suggests. Many are in their breeding plumage and will either have wintered locally or will be staging migrants.

The grey non-breeding individuals are second-calendar year birds that will not breed until the following year, and will probably spend the summer locally. There is a small group of grey non-breeding Red Knots towards the top left-hand corner of the image. Norfolk, UK, mid April.

[Lower right] Eurasian Curlews roosting at high tide. Standing on one leg, the other folded into the breast feathers, and with bills tucked into their scapulars, they are minimising heat loss and thus conserving energy. Cornwall, UK, mid September.

LOAFING BEHAVIOUR

In many shorebird flocks there will be birds that are roosting, but others, largely quiescent, just standing or perhaps indulging in an occasional half-hearted preen – this is 'loafing'. Occasionally loafing shorebirds will simply squat on their tarsi. They don't preen, they don't sleep, they just sit. This behaviour often seems to occur when the conditions are hot, and so presumably it is a means of cooling. The plumage is held tight to the body to minimise its insulation properties, allowing any breeze to help the cooling process. In similar circumstances they may also simply sit, perhaps losing heat to the ground. Shorebirds will also pant to loose heat, particularly in the tropics.

ANTI-PREDATOR DISPLAYS

Predators are inevitably attracted to shorebird flocks. The arrival of a predator will often result in coordinated, murmuration-like mass flights as the birds attempt to avoid its attentions. A flock of shorebirds that is disturbed by a predator will usually take flight, but single birds will often react to the passage of a raptor overhead or to the sudden appearance of a potential non-aerial predator, such a human or a dog, by crouching motionless until the danger seems to have passed, after which they usually continue feeding.

DISTRACTION DISPLAYS

Some shorebirds have interesting distraction displays, particularly woodcocks and snipe, that are used in different circumstances, including the distraction of possible predators and as an aggressive display to territorial intruders. It seems likely that all woodcocks and snipes may perform these displays given the appropriate circumstances, although the displays have only been described for some species.

A Common Snipe giving this distraction will face away from the perceived disturbance, crouch with its body close to the ground, holding tail feathers fanned upward, just forward of vertical, and with its head low and bill resting along the ground. It gives the impression that it is perhaps inviting a potential predator to strike at its tail, but when seen from either front or back there are prominent eye-like black spots towards the tips of the central tail feathers. This

[Upper left] Roosting Red Knots at high tide. Part of a flock of about 4,000–5,000, almost all non-breeding birds that spend the summer along the north Norfolk coast or in The Wash. Red Knots do not breed until they are two-years old, and nearly all of these birds are first-years in grey non-breeding plumage. There are a few red birds in breeding plumage, probably failed breeders that have already returned from the high arctic. Norfolk, UK, late June.

[Lower left] A small group of loafing and roosting Sanderlings. Most are doing some desultory preening, but some are roosting. A mix of first-calendar year birds and adults, all in non-breeding plumage. Norfolk, UK, late March.

[Above] Roosting juvenile Dunlins. Six birds hidden amongst rocks just above the high-tide line, tucked up and barely visible to the casual observer, but all with at least half an eye open. Cornwall, UK, mid September.

Loafing shorebirds

[Left] Loafing Wilson's Plover. An example of a shorebird sitting on its tarsi. Florida, USA, mid May.

[Middle] Loafing shorebirds, trying to keep cool. The two Short-billed Dowitchers in the foreground are reacting to the late morning heat either by sitting down (presumably the ground is relatively cool) or by squatting on its tarsi to take advantage of the cooling effect of any breeze. Both birds are minimising the insulating effect of their plumage by pulling in their body feathers. The birds behind are another dowitcher and a Red Knot. Apart from the squatting dowitcher (which is in breeding plumage – perhaps a failed breeder or one that has not made the journey to its breeding grounds), they are second calendar-year non-breeding birds. Florida, USA, late June.

[Below] Double-banded Courser. Panting to keep cool. Namibia, late December.

[Right] Pied Avocet mobbing a female Marsh Harrier. At this site Marsh Harriers are major predators of Pied Avocet chicks. A raptor flying over will usually put a feeding shorebird flock to flight, but individuals will often crouch, motionless, until the danger has passed. Norfolk, UK, late June.

[Middle] Merlin *Falco columbarius*, a regular predator of shorebirds. Moments earlier this bird had attacked a nearby small group of three or four Western Sandpipers. Its attack was unsuccessful, but it came so close to me that it almost passed through the legs of the camera tripod before landing on the bank just a few metres away. Salton Sea, south California, USA, early November.

[Below] Peregrine Falcon *Falco peregrinus*, another regular shorebird predator. As I watched from a distance, this bird made an unsuccessful attack on a large flock of Red Knots. It landed quite close to a large roosting group of Great Cormorants *Phalacrocoracidae carbo* and remained there until it was disturbed by another bird photographer, less patient than myself! Norfolk, UK, late December.

distraction display occurs when the snipe is on the ground or other perch and is startled by another bird flying past unexpectedly, or by a nearby human observer. The aggressive display to another snipe is similar, but the bird faces the intruder.

The Eurasian Woodcock has a somewhat similar display to the Common Snipe, probably used in similar circumstances, but because of its nocturnal and rather secretive lifestyle this is poorly described. Again, the display involves the raised and fanned tail, although with Eurasian Woodcock the pale-tipped tail feathers are darker above, but bright iridescent white below, which results in a very striking effect when seen from behind.

EFFECT OF PREDATORS ON SHOREBIRD FLOCKS

Two studies of the predation of wintering shorebird flocks provide an interesting comparison of sites and scale. The first was carried out over two winter periods (although more intensely in the second year) at the 4.5 km² Bolinas Lagoon, Point Reyes, California, USA. The lagoon is tidal, is separated from the Pacific by a low sand-spit and has extensive sand and mudflats. During the survey the wintering population of shorebirds was about 5,400, the most numerous species being Dunlin (1,900 birds) and Least Sandpiper (1,600 birds). Other shorebirds present, but in smaller numbers, were Sanderling (130 birds) and Western Sandpiper (350 birds). The major predators were a single Merlin *Falco columbarius* and several Short-eared Owls *Asio flammeus*, although other species were also involved, particularly during cold weather when predation increased. Over the second winter of the study predators took 21% of the Dunlins, 12% of the Least Sandpipers, 7.5% of the Western Sandpipers and 13.5% of the Sanderlings. The Merlin's success rate was highest for single birds (25.6% of attacks), much less (7–8%) for flocks of two to 49 birds, but increased again (to 21.4%) if the flock size was greater than 50 birds, although the reasons for this are not clear.

The second study is more recent and on a larger scale, in terms of both time and area. The Parc National du Banc d'Arguin on the coast of Mauritania, west Africa, is an extensive coastal area of open shallow sea and tidal mudflats, salt plains and desert. It

[Opposite] Three shorebirds, all crouching in alarm, all reacting in a similar way to potential predators. The Dotterel [top] (juvenile, Cornwall, UK, mid September) has been disturbed by a dog, but the Common Snipe [middle] (adult, Norfolk, UK, early August) and Common Redshank [bottom] (adult non-breeding, Norfolk, UK, late March) are both reacting to overflying Marsh Harriers.

[Right] Presumed anti-predator display by an adult Common Snipe, probably given as an instinctive response to my presence in a nearby hide, although I was trying to be as quiet and inconspicuous as possible. It displayed like this three times over a couple of minutes, each display lasting less than a couple of seconds. The eye-like black-spot on the tail is conspicuous. Norfolk, UK, early August.

is used in the northern winter by about 30% of the shorebirds of the East Atlantic Flyway. The survey concentrated on a small portion of the Parc, an area of 50 km² of which about 22 km² are tidal mudflats. The major predators of shorebirds here are Lanner *Falco biarmicus*, Barbary *F. pelegrinoides* and Peregrine Falcon *F. peregrinus*. The study, over five winters, found that the larger shorebird flocks (those of more than 1,000 birds) were attacked by these large falcons less often than were smaller flocks, particularly the flocks of less than 50 birds.

Most vulnerable were the species that feed relatively close to the shore, and did so in small flocks. With Bar-tailed Godwit, Red Knot and Dunlin, the juveniles were considerably more at risk than adults. On average, just 0.1% of the adult Red Knots were killed each winter, compared to 1% of the juveniles who tended to forage earlier and later in the tidal cycle than the adults, and were closer to shore and more vulnerable to surprise attacks. The annual survival rate of Red Knots could also be estimated from an individual colour-marking programme, which showed that predation by falcons at the Banc d'Arguin was responsible for about 6% of annual mortality of the juveniles and about 1% of the adults. Clearly, although the Californian study did not consider the age of the shorebirds, predation was more severe there, presumably reflecting the smaller flocks and the smaller area involved, which allowed more opportunity for surprise attack by the predators. The much lower predation rates at the extensive Banc d'Arguin shows that there can be survival value in making the long migration to an extensive non-breeding area, quite apart from the value of the food supply that the area provides.

FLOCKING FOR FEEDING - INLAND SPECIES

It is much less usual to find flocks of shorebirds inland, but flocks occur outside the breeding season if feeding conditions at some individual location become particularly favourable. In Europe, ephemeral flocking by Northern Lapwing and European Golden Plover are the most obvious examples and, as discussed in Chapter 3, such flocks may feed at night. Flocking will help to reduce their vulnerability to gulls stealing food.

[Above] Ephemeral flocking – a 'wisp' (the collective noun for a flight of snipe) of Common Snipe disturbed from a wet meadow. The drainage ditches at this site have deliberately been blocked to raise the water table with the intention of making the habitat suitable for such species as Common Snipe and Common Redshank. The success of this scheme is shown here, with 31 birds in the wisp that are attracted to the improved food supply provided by this seasonal wetland. The photo also gives a good impression of the habitat. Northamptonshire, UK, mid November.

[Opposite, upper right] Anti-predator display by Eurasian Woodcock. Woodcock have a similar display to that shown by Common Snipe in the following images, but on this occasion it was rather half-hearted – it simply raised its tail while facing away from me, before walking off into the vegetation behind. Northamptonshire, UK, mid January.

[Opposite, lower right] Eurasian Woodcock tail feathers showing the pale tips that are rather dull above, but beneath are an iridescent bright white, which catch both the eye and the light from a flashgun (as seen in the previous image). Two central tail feathers are shown, upper surface (left) and lower surface (right).

Snipe on wet grassland provide another example of ephemeral flocking, which occurs when high ground-water levels drive worms and other invertebrates close to the ground surface, and at the same time provide a soft substrate that is easily probed. Snipe will often feed at night under these conditions and roost in the same area during the day. Quite large numbers of snipe can occur in such conditions, although the birds will move on again if the water level continues to rise and flooding occurs.

REFERENCES

Attanasi, A., Cavagna, A., Del Castello, L., Giardina, I., Grigera, T.S., Jelić, A., Melillo, S., Parisi, L., Pohl, O., Shen, E. and Viale, M., 2014. Superfluid transport of information in turning flocks of starlings. *Nature Physics* **10** (9), 691–696.

Cavagna, A., Giardina, I., Parisi, G., Santagati, R., Stefanini, F. and Viale, M., 2010. Scale-free correlations in starling flocks. *Proceedings of the National Academy of Sciences*, **107** (26), 11865–11870.

Page, G. and Whitacre, D.F., 1975. Raptor predation on wintering shorebirds. *Condor* **77**, 73–83.

van den Hout, P.J., Spaans, B. and Piersma, T., 2008. Differential mortality of wintering shorebirds on the Banc d'Arguin, Mauritania, due to predation by large falcons. *Ibis* **150** (Suppl. 1), 219–230.

This list is a slightly modified version of the IOC's list. English names used in this book that differ from the IOC list are given in parentheses. Subspecies are not listed, although races identifiable in the field are named in the figure captions. Unnumbered species marked † are either extinct or are presumed so.

Genus	Species no.	
1 Buttonquails	1–16	*Turnix* spp.
2 Quail-plover	17	Quail-plover *Ortyxelos meiffrenii*
3 Stone-curlews, Thick-knees	18	Eurasian Stone-curlew *Burhinus oedicnemus*
	19	Indian Stone-curlew *Burhinus indicus*
	20	Senegal Thick-knee *Burhinus senegalensis*
	21	Water Thick-knee *Burhinus vermiculatus*
	22	Spotted Thick-knee *Burhinus capensis*
	23	Double-striped Thick-knee *Burhinus bistriatus*
	24	Peruvian Thick-knee *Burhinus superciliaris*
	25	Bush Stone-curlew *Burhinus grallarius*
4	26	Great Stone-curlew *Esacus recurvirostris*
	27	Beach Stone-curlew *Esacus magnirostris*
5 Sheathbills	28	Snowy Sheathbill *Chionis albus*
	29	Black-faced Sheathbill *Chionis minor*
6 Magellanic Plover	30	Magellanic Plover *Pluvianellus socialis*
7 Oystercatchers	31	Magellanic Oystercatcher *Haematopus leucopodus*
	32	Blackish Oystercatcher *Haematopus ater*
	33	(American) Black Oystercatcher *Haematopus bachmani*
	34	American Oystercatcher *Haematopus palliatus*
	–	Canary Islands Oystercatcher *Haematopus meadewaldoi* †
	35	African (Black) Oystercatcher *Haematopus moquini*
	36	Eurasian Oystercatcher *Haematopus ostralegus*
	37	South Island (Pied) Oystercatcher *Haematopus finschi*
	38	(Australian) Pied Oystercatcher *Haematopus longirostris*
	39	Variable Oystercatcher *Haematopus unicolor*
	40	Chatham Oystercatcher *Haematopus chathamensis*
	41	Sooty Oystercatcher *Haematopus fuliginosus*
8 Crab-plover	42	Crab-plover *Dromas ardeola*
9 Ibisbill	43	Ibisbill *Ibidorhyncha struthersii*
10 Stilts, Avocets	44	Black-winged Stilt *Himantopus himantopus*
	45	Australasian Pied/White-headed Stilt *Himantopus leucocephalus*

Genus	Species no.	
	46	Black-necked Stilt *Himantopus mexicanus*
	47	White-backed Stilt *Himantopus melanurus*
	48	Black Stilt *Himantopus novaezelandiae*
11	49	Banded Stilt *Cladorhynchus leucocephalus*
12	50	Pied Avocet *Recurvirostra avosetta*
	51	American Avocet *Recurvirostra americana*
	52	Red-necked Avocet *Recurvirostra novaehollandiae*
	53	Andean Avocet *Recurvirostra andina*
13 Lapwings	54	Northern Lapwing *Vanellus vanellus*
	55	Long-toed Lapwing *Vanellus crassirostris*
	56	Blacksmith Lapwing *Vanellus armatus*
	57	Spur-winged Lapwing *Vanellus spinosus*
	58	River Lapwing *Vanellus duvaucelii*
	59	Black-headed Lapwing *Vanellus tectus*
	60	Yellow-wattled Lapwing *Vanellus malabaricus*
	61	White-crowned Lapwing *Vanellus albiceps*
	62	Senegal Lapwing *Vanellus lugubris*
	63	Black-winged Lapwing *Vanellus melanopterus*
	64	Crowned Lapwing *Vanellus coronatus*
	65	African Wattled Lapwing *Vanellus senegallus*
	66	Spot-breasted Lapwing *Vanellus melanocephalus*
	67	Brown-chested Lapwing *Vanellus superciliosus*
	68	Grey-headed Lapwing *Vanellus cinereus*
	69	Red-wattled Lapwing *Vanellus indicus*
	–	Javan Lapwing *Vanellus macropterus* †
	70	Banded Lapwing *Vanellus tricolor*
	71	Masked Lapwing *Vanellus miles*
	72	Sociable Lapwing *Vanellus gregarius*
	73	White-tailed Lapwing *Vanellus leucurus*
	74	Southern Lapwing *Vanellus chilensis*
	75	Andean Lapwing *Vanellus resplendens*
14 Plovers	76	Red-kneed Dotterel *Erythrogonys cinctus*
15	77	Inland Dotterel *Peltohyas australis*
16	78	Wrybill *Anarhynchus frontalis*
17	79	European Golden Plover *Pluvialis apricaria*
	80	Pacific Golden Plover *Pluvialis fulva*

Genus	Species no.	
	81	American Golden Plover *Pluvialis dominica*
	82	Grey (Black-bellied) Plover *Pluvialis squatarola*
18	83	New Zealand Dotterel/Plover *Charadrius obscurus*
	84	Common Ringed Plover *Charadrius hiaticula*
	85	Semipalmated Plover *Charadrius semipalmatus*
	86	Long-billed Plover *Charadrius placidus*
	87	Little Ringed Plover *Charadrius dubius*
	88	Wilson's Plover *Charadrius wilsonia*
	89	Killdeer *Charadrius vociferus*
	90	Piping Plover *Charadrius melodus*
	91	Madagascan Plover *Charadrius thoracicus*
	92	Kittlitz's Plover *Charadrius pecuarius*
	93	St Helena Plover *Charadrius sanctaehelenae*
	94	Three-banded Plover *Charadrius tricollaris*
	95	Forbes's Plover *Charadrius forbesi*
	96	White-fronted Plover *Charadrius marginatus*
	97	Kentish Plover *Charadrius alexandrinus*
	98	Snowy Plover *Charadrius nivosus*
	99	Javan Plover *Charadrius javanicus*
	100	Red-capped Plover *Charadrius ruficapillus*
	101	Malaysian Plover *Charadrius peronii*
	102	Chestnut-banded Plover *Charadrius pallidus*
	103	Collared Plover *Charadrius collaris*
	104	Puna Plover *Charadrius alticola*
	105	Two-banded Plover *Charadrius falklandicus*
	106	Double-banded Plover *Charadrius bicinctus*
	107	Lesser Sand Plover *Charadrius mongolus*
	108	Greater Sand Plover *Charadrius leschenaultii*
	109	Caspian Plover *Charadrius asiaticus*
	110	Oriental Plover *Charadrius veredus*
	111	Eurasian Dotterel *Charadrius morinellus*
	112	Rufous-chested Dotterel/Plover *Charadrius modestus*
	113	Mountain Plover *Charadrius montanus*
19	114	Hooded Plover (Dotterel) *Thinornis (rubricollis) cucullatus*
	115	Shore Plover (Dotterel) *Thinornis novaeseelandiae*
20	116	Black-fronted Dotterel *Elseyornis melanops*
21	117	Tawny-throated Dotterel *Oreopholus ruficollis*
22	118	Diademed Sandpiper-plover *Phegornis mitchellii*
23	119	Pied Plover *Hoploxypterus (Vanellus) cayanus*
24	120	Egyptian Plover *Pluvianus aegyptius*
25 Painted-snipes	121	Greater Painted-snipe *Rostratula benghalensis*
	122	Australian Painted-snipe *Rostratula australis*

Genus	Species no.	
26	123	South American Painted-snipe *Nycticryphes semicollaris*
27 Jacanas	124	Lesser Jacana *Microparra capensis*
28	125	African Jacana *Actophilornis africanus*
	126	Madagascan Jacana *Actophilornis albinucha*
29	127	Comb-crested Jacana *Irediparra gallinacea*
30	128	Pheasant-tailed Jacana *Hydrophasianus chirurgus*
31	129	Bronze-winged Jacana *Metopidius indicus*
32	130	Northern Jacana *Jacana spinosa*
	131	Wattled Jacana *Jacana jacana*
33 Plains-wanderer	132	Plains-wanderer *Pedionomus torquatus*
34 Seedsnipes	133	Rufous-bellied Seedsnipe *Attagis gayi*
	134	White-bellied Seedsnipe *Attagis malouinus*
35	135	Grey-breasted Seedsnipe *Thinocorus orbignyianus*
	136	Least Seedsnipe *Thinocorus rumicivorus*
36 Woodcocks	137	Eurasian Woodcock *Scolopax rusticola*
	138	Amami Woodcock *Scolopax mira*
	139	Javan Woodcock *Scolopax saturata*
	140	New Guinea Woodcock *Scolopax rosenbergii*
	141	Bukidnon Woodcock *Scolopax bukidnonensis*
	142	Sulawesi Woodcock *Scolopax celebensis*
	143	Moluccan Woodcock *Scolopax rochussenii*
	144	American Woodcock *Scolopax minor*
37 Snipes	145	Chatham Snipe *Coenocorypha pusilla*
	–	North Island Snipe *Coenocorypha barrierensis* †
	–	South Island Snipe *Coenocorypha iredalei* †
	146	Snares Snipe *Coenocorypha huegeli*
	147	Subantarctic Snipe *Coenocorypha aucklandica*
38	148	Jack Snipe *Lymnocryptes minimus*
39	149	Solitary Snipe *Gallinago solitaria*
	150	Latham's/Japanese Snipe *Gallinago hardwickii*
	151	Wood Snipe *Gallinago nemoricola*
	152	Pin-tailed Snipe *Gallinago stenura*
	153	Swinhoe's Snipe *Gallinago megala*
	154	African Snipe *Gallinago nigripennis*
	155	Madagascan Snipe *Gallinago macrodactyla*
	156	Great Snipe *Gallinago media*
	157	Common Snipe *Gallinago gallinago*
	158	Wilson's Snipe *Gallinago delicata*
	159	South American Snipe *Gallinago paraguaiae*
	160	Puna Snipe *Gallinago andina*
	161	Noble Snipe *Gallinago nobilis*
	162	Giant Snipe *Gallinago undulata*
	163	Fuegian Snipe *Gallinago stricklandii*

Genus	Species no.	
	164	Jameson's Snipe *Gallinago jamesoni*
	165	Imperial Snipe *Gallinago imperialis*
40 Dowitchers	166	Short-billed Dowitcher *Limnodromus griseus*
	167	Long-billed Dowitcher *Limnodromus scolopaceus*
	168	Asian Dowitcher *Limnodromus semipalmatus*
41 Godwits	169	Black-tailed Godwit *Limosa limosa*
	170	Hudsonian Godwit *Limosa haemastica*
	171	Bar-tailed Godwit *Limosa lapponica*
	172	Marbled Godwit *Limosa fedoa*
42 Curlews	173	Little Curlew *Numenius minutus*
	--	Eskimo Curlew *Numenius borealis* †
	174	Whimbrel *Numenius phaeopus*
	175	Bristle-thighed Curlew *Numenius tahitiensis*
	176	Slender-billed Curlew *Numenius tenuirostris*
	177	Eurasian Curlew *Numenius arquata*
	178	Far Eastern Curlew *Numenius madagascariensis*
	179	Long-billed Curlew *Numenius americanus*
43	180	Upland Sandpiper *Bartramia longicauda*
44 Sandpipers	181	Spotted Redshank *Tringa erythropus*
	182	Common Redshank *Tringa totanus*
	183	Marsh Sandpiper *Tringa stagnatilis*
	184	Common Greenshank *Tringa nebularia*
	185	Nordmann's Greenshank *Tringa guttifer*
	186	Greater Yellowlegs *Tringa melanoleuca*
	187	Lesser Yellowlegs *Tringa flavipes*
	188	Green Sandpiper *Tringa ochropus*
	189	Solitary Sandpiper *Tringa solitaria*
	190	Wood Sandpiper *Tringa glareola*
	191	Grey-tailed Tattler *Tringa brevipes*
	192	Wandering Tattler *Tringa incana*
	193	Willet *Tringa semipalmata*
45	194	Terek Sandpiper *Xenus cinereus*
46	195	Common Sandpiper *Actitis hypoleucos*
	196	Spotted Sandpiper *Actitis macularius*
47	197	Tuamotu Sandpiper *Prosobonia parvirostris*
	–	Kiritimati Sandpiper *Prosobonia cancellata* †
	–	Tahiti Sandpiper *Prosobonia leucoptera* †
	–	Moorea Sandpiper *Prosobonia ellisi* †
48	198	Ruddy Turnstone *Arenaria interpres*
	199	Black Turnstone *Arenaria melanocephala*
49	200	Surfbird *Aphriza virgata*
50	201	Great Knot *Calidris tenuirostris*
	202	Red Knot *Calidris canutus*

Genus	Species no.	
	203	Sanderling *Calidris alba*
	204	Semipalmated Sandpiper *Calidris pusilla*
	205	Western Sandpiper *Calidris mauri*
	206	Red-necked Stint *Calidris ruficollis*
	207	Little Stint *Calidris minuta*
	208	Temminck's Stint *Calidris temminckii*
	219	Long-toed Stint *Calidris subminuta*
	210	Least Sandpiper *Calidris minutilla*
	211	White-rumped Sandpiper *Calidris fuscicollis*
	212	Baird's Sandpiper *Calidris bairdii*
	213	Pectoral Sandpiper *Calidris melanotos*
	214	Sharp-tailed Sandpiper *Calidris acuminata*
	215	Curlew Sandpiper *Calidris ferruginea*
	216	Purple Sandpiper *Calidris maritima*
	217	Rock Sandpiper *Calidris ptilocnemis*
	218	Dunlin *Calidris alpina*
	219	Stilt Sandpiper *Calidris himantopus*
51	220	Spoon-billed Sandpiper *Eurynorhynchus pygmeus*
52	221	Broad-billed Sandpiper *Limicola falcinellus*
53	222	Buff-breasted Sandpiper *Tryngites subruficollis*
54	223	Ruff *Philomachus pugnax*
55	224	Wilson's Phalarope *Phalaropus tricolor*
	225	Red-necked Phalarope *Phalaropus lobatus*
	226	Grey/Red Phalarope *Phalaropus fulicarius*
56 Coursers	227	Cream-colored Courser *Cursorius cursor*
	228	Somali Courser *Cursorius somalensis*
	229	Burchell's Courser *Cursorius rufus*
	230	Temminck's Courser *Cursorius temminckii*
	231	Indian Courser *Cursorius coromandelicus*
57	232	Double-banded Courser *Rhinoptilus africanus*
	233	Three-banded (Heuglin's) Courser *Rhinoptilus cinctus*
	234	Bronze-winged Courser *Rhinoptilus chalcopterus*
	235	Jerdon's Courser *Rhinoptilus bitorquatus*
58 Pratincoles	236	Australian Pratincole *Stiltia isabella*
59	237	Collared Pratincole *Glareola pratincola*
	238	Oriental Pratincole *Glareola maldivarum*
	239	Black-winged Pratincole *Glareola nordmanni*
	240	Madagascan Pratincole *Glareola ocularis*
	241	Rock Pratincole *Glareola nuchalis*
	242	Grey Pratincole *Glareola cinerea*
	243	Small Pratincole *Glareola lactea*

The scientific names of the shorebirds are not given here, but can be found in the Appendix. Photographs are shown in *italics*. **Bold** entries refer to pages containing general information and are thus placed before the detail of particular species.